FROM THE HART

*A Collection of Favorite Columns on Love, Loss,
Marriage (and Other Extreme Sports)*

BETSY HART

Cover photo by Jackie Chindblom
Cover design by Jones House Creative

ISBN-10: 0615608841
EAN-13: 9780615608846

For my Tom
Really, God? Really?

FROM THE HART

Contents

The Backstory of From the Hart

Chapter One

The Study of Love   1

Romance: Better Living Through Chemistry?   3
"Soul Mates"? Schmoul Mates! Looking for Love in all the Wrong Places   6
David Cassidy, Teens, and Lessons on Love   9
Divorce — A Personal Report (and a Little Advice) from the Trenches   12
The Dangers of Romantic Pornography   15
Time to Value a Different Kind of Valentine?   18
Why a Remake of Roman Holiday *(and* Casablanca*) Would Sadly Have Happier Endings Today*   21
Love Potion Number 9 — It May be All About the Dopamine   24

Chapter Two

What Ever Happened to Courtship?   27

If He Wants You He'll Pursue You   30
How "I Am Woman Hear Me Roar" Hurts Real Women   33
Dating After Divorce: Some Different Rules for this Single Mom   36
Time to Take the Online Dating Plunge   39
"Suitor" Beats "Boyfriend" for the Marriage Minded   42
Girls Don't (Shouldn't) Call Boys   45

Chapter Three

A Little Advice (A Lot of Advice) for the Marriage Minded, Newlyweds, and Just About Everyone Else　49

"All About Me" Weddings Are Nothing to Celebrate!　51
Bride and Groom - Now Hear This:
(Your Wedding Guests Will Be Glad You Did)　54
Hey Newlyweds, Listen Up! The Wedding is Over Now it's all About the Marriage　57
Wives, Time to Lighten Up on Your Guy?　60
What Men Want (And It's Not JUST What You Think)　62
For the Sake of the Kids Make Your Spouse Your Priority　66

Chapter Four

Why Marriage Matters　69

Rising Rates of Single Parenthood: Putting Moms and Kids at Risk　72
Easy Relationships Offer No Paradise　75
Living Together Outside of Marriage? Grow up!　78
Falling Marriage Rates: Uh-oh Watch Out Below　81
Who Needs Marriage? I Do!　84
The Case for Short Courtships and Marrying Young - Really　86
What if the Purpose of Marriage is Holiness, Not Just Happiness?　90

Chapter Five

Why Divorce Matters　93

When the Church Abandons the Marriages in its Midst　95
From a Single Mom - It's Supposed to Take a Family to Raise a Child　98
*Why Choosing to Leave a Spouse Means Choosing to
Leave a Family, Too*　101
Telling the Truth to Kids About Divorce? It's Not That Complicated!　104
*Divorce - Five Years Later, and Learning a Little Resiliency
Goes a Long Way*　107

Chapter Six

From The Other Woman to A Marriage Transformed　111

Only After Marriage do Cheating Rules Apply　113
Life is Short, So "Have an Affair" or "Work on Your Marriage"?　116
Meeting The Other Woman　119
An Affair to Forget　122
An Update on Casey: Her Married Boyfriend Divorces　125
The Story of a Marriage Redeemed?　128
A Conclusion, But No Clarity, in Casey's Affair　130
"Denise" and Marriage: A Story of Grace　133
Divorce — It Can't Happen To Me! Only, It Did　136
Getting a Second Chance at First Love　139

Acknowledgements　143

About Betsy Hart　145

Contact Information　147

The Backstory of
From the Hart

There's a story going around about the woman who goes to the "Find a Husband" department store. On every floor she has the chance to accept who is there, or go up one level where the men get better. But, she can't go back. So, by level two all the men have stopped playing Xbox in their parents' basements, and have jobs. By level four she finds that the fellows are also good looking, make good money, and want to be really involved dads. By level seven they are all that and sensitive and share their feelings too. But at floor nine a sign greets the woman that says, "You are woman 8,395,207 to reach this floor. There are no men here, the floor exists to show that women are impossible to please."

Across the street, a man goes to the "Find a Wife" department store. By level two he finds women who keep themselves nice looking, and like sex and beer. Finally, he decides to ask what is on floor three. He's told that no one knows.

Sure, the story sells both men and women more than a little short. But it still captures the flavor of something I think we see too often today: That when it comes to men and matters of the heart, too many women ask for too much, but settle for too little.

This is what I mean: I see women essentially holding out for the caricatures of men that they see in chick flicks. "Romantic pornography" I call such films. You know, the super sensitive male, always talking about his feelings. A man who tearfully talks about the "magic" he felt when in the presence of his wife, ala Tom Hanks in *Sleepless in Seattle*. A man created in the image of woman.

Here women ask for too much. Ironically, it's probably not what women want in a real life fellow anyway.

What so few women seem to insist upon, though, is a real suitor. A good man who *wants* the woman he loves to know that she is wanted. Whether or not there are flowers or love notes or magic involved, it will simply be natural for him to make sure she is secure in his honest intentions of marriage for her. Everything about their relationship will be moving toward that obvious conclusion in a timely way.

That's real, manly pursuit, and the kind I see fewer and fewer women expecting however much they might want and hope for it. Not only do they not have such legitimate expectations, most women will make themselves sexually available to men without marriage at all, whether or not they want to. Why? Because while women have put aside the once natural presumption that a relationship ought to progress toward marriage, men and our culture have firmly established the expectation that women will make themselves sexually available to men outside of marriage. It's all a little ironic. And surely, it's one reason marriage rates are plummeting in our culture.

In this, women are settling for too little. And yes, though we might not see it as clearly, men are too.

It all has huge implications for men, women, children and our society.

This is one theme that emerged as I gathered some three dozen of my favorite columns written in the years since I became (suddenly) single, and a single mom to four young kids, in 2004.

But there are other themes that show themselves too. One is that we increasingly see romantic love, and certainly marriage, as something private and between just the two people involved. But of course that's never really the case. As humans we are built to have interconnected relationships. So even our most intimate are not really "all about me" or even "all about us." Yet more and more our culture preaches just the opposite. And that affects all of us too.

It seems to me these themes are more than a little intertwined.

So then, in time for the traditional wedding season of summer, I include here columns on love, romance, marriage and the loss of it, wedding etiquette, and a little insight into George Clooney - and men like him. In the pages that follow you'll find essays in which I wrote about Valentine's Day, the chemistry of romance and why, when it comes to chasing the highs of love, we are setting our sights too low. I've offered advice to newlyweds (sex really matters and wives, please don't try to turn your husband into your best girlfriend!); lamented the lost art of courtship; and delved into the backstory of relationships both rocked by and redeemed from infidelity.

Through my columns, which I often call "conversations," I've chronicled my own divorce and life as a single mom, and have heard from so many readers with similar stories who felt a little more supported when I told my own. These columns include one I wrote when the divorce was still fairly new (reading it now it's clear the shock had not yet worn off); five years later when life was unfolding for my kids and me in unexpected ways; and later still a victory of sorts when I forgot altogether, until it had passed, the anniversary of the day my then-husband decided to walk out the door of our family life for good.

What I wrote at the conclusion of that first column about the end of my marriage — that God's mercies are new every morning — proved especially true in so much of what I lived and wrote about after. And so that earliest column is placed almost last so perhaps one says, "and so it was."

But it's not quite last. Recently I added my favorite column of all, and one of a handful not in the original electronic version of *From the Hart*. "Getting a Second Chance at First Love" was written after I became engaged, earlier this year, to a man I am quite simply crazy about. As I like to tell Tom, he's not just the one I've been waiting for these last several years. He's the one I've been waiting for my whole life! But is he my "soul mate"? Well, I talk a little about that too.

Life sure is full of surprises. I am glad I didn't give up hoping for this one.

Whatever I write, it's always something I'm passionate about. But it wouldn't mean anything except that often readers have kindly told me that what I've written touches them, and even speaks to what they are going through in some way too. I am so grateful for that. And that's why I keep putting "conversations" on a page.

From the Hart: Love, Loss, Marriage (and Other Extreme Sports) is a collection of my columns all written as a single mother with four school-aged kids, yet with a consistent sensibility that men and women are wonderfully different and we really do need each other; that marriage and family matter profoundly; and that real romance is so much more and different than anything portrayed in the typical romantic comedy. Is it ironic that I've written so much on romance, courtship, and marriage over the years as a woman surprised by a divorce myself? I'll let you decide. I do know that far from being jaded, I believe in all these wonderful things more than ever. And that was true even before I met Tom. Maybe that's what made me able to love again. And maybe I've even had some insights because of my loss, too. God surely works in mysterious ways.

About the Text: Perhaps because I recently lived a love story myself, I've organized the columns I've included here a little bit like a love story too. First is the romance and courtship, of course, then a little about weddings; the meaning and significance of marriage; the trials, and joys, of same; and tales of divorce and stories of infidelity - and redemption. Including in my case, finding love again. Like any good romance, at least in real life, the progression of the story here is at times a little chaotic. I hope it helps that I've included chapter notes, intro-ducing groups of columns, as the story progresses.

All of the columns included in this collection were distrib-uted by Scripps Howard News Service to its client newspapers around the country on the date noted on the column here. Scripps Howard graciously and generously gave me the right to use the columns for this collection, and gave me access to its extensive archives. I am very appreciative.

The titles included here, though, are not typically those under which the columns were distributed, titles which news-papers themselves often change anyway. These titles were gen-erally created by me to convey the content from my perspective.

The columns themselves are generally (but not always) reproduced here as they were distributed by Scripps Howard News. In some cases if a cultural reference would no longer be obvious, or to clarify meaning or focus, or perhaps just clean up a sentence that now seems messy - I have edited some columns.

Some of these essays are very personal, some challenge the culture at large. But I promise you they are all, well, from the heart. Thank you for letting me share them with you.

CHAPTER ONE

❧

The Study of Love

The course of true love never did run smooth.

- William Shakespeare

The columns that follow have a great deal to do with romantic love. Our culture loves the obsession of love. I find the study of love fascinating. And I found it so long before I found love again. Is love about actions, or feelings, or both - and if there is a difference does it matter anyway? I, for one, think how we view love matters a great deal in terms of whether or not we will be satisfied with the love we find. And the love we express. The fact that more and more science is discovering that many feelings of love have chemical underpinnings suggests to me, yet again, that God works in very wonderful and mysterious ways.

But I'm concerned that if in romance we yearn for love to look a certain way and always with a "soul mate" - and our culture certainly encourages just that - might we miss a deeper, more lasting variety of love with a partner? If we think romantic love always has to have a storybook ending, ala what I call "romantic pornography," might we sometimes be missing the real life love that is right in front of us?

I wonder if in so many ways we settle for too little. The shiny object that grabs our attention in the moment but can't really satisfy, instead of the real and more valuable but sometimes less obvious gem. It's certainly clear which one our culture encourages. I don't think I have all the answers and of course I don't think the columns that follow have, or will, change the culture. But if they change the culture of just one relationship a little bit for the better? Well, I will be grateful.

Romance: Better Living Through Chemistry?

February 9, 2006

With Valentine's Day set for Tuesday, one may wonder, is love in the air?

For starters, it seems like it's mostly in the brain.

At least that's what Lauren Slater writes in *National Geographic* in a fascinating February cover piece, simply titled, "Love."

"For the first time, new research has begun to illuminate where love lies in the brain, the particulars of its chemical components ..." According to Slater, "scientists say that the brain chemistry of infatuation is akin to mental illness - which gives new meaning to the term 'madly in love.' "

Anthropologist Helen Fisher has spent years looking for love, only not in bars or with want ads, but with an MRI machine. She and her colleagues found couples who had been wildly in love for about seven months. They put each person into a brain scanner and showed each half of the couple a picture, one neutral, the other of their beloved.

Watch out. In the latter case, "the parts of the brain linked to reward and pleasure ... lit up." What Fisher found, and what most amazed her, was that the chemical pathways to the part of the brain where love resided, so to speak, ignited a dense spread of receptors for a powerful neurotransmitter known as dopamine. Or, better put, the brain released its very own Love Potion Number 9.

So then there's a reason why, Slater reports, when you are newly in love, "you can stay up all night, watch the sun rise, run a race, ski fast down a slope ordinarily too steep for your skill ... " And that feeling is wonderful. It's also, as the magazine notes, almost always fleeting.

Physically that rush of love can't be maintained over time. Imagine if it could. What would have happened to civilization? Who would have had time to build it?

One theory is that we simply build up a resistance to the "high" of dopamine. So then true love goes into a different form. In a way it settles down, and it's based more on con-nections - marriage, children, commitments. We finally emerge from our "high" state to see that something exists, must exist, beyond just the two of us.

I remember, long before I was married, being captivated when I read about this transformation in romantic love as described by writer C.S. Lewis. He talked about it in more than one of his books as a more profound, deep, and satisfying kind of love than the original, if delightful, thrall.

That is, if we accept that transition with our beloved.

And so the science seems to back up what has been intui-tively known through the ages. Consider the biblical passage from First Corinthians so often read at weddings: "Love is patient, love is kind ... love does not act unbecomingly ..." Bottom line? For love to be lasting and true, at some level it has to be about action and deed, not just feelings.

Yet beautifully, those actions and deeds may produce their own love chemical - and joy - though of a different sort. In contrast to the "high" of dopamine, Slater reveals that oxytocin is a chemical "that promotes bonding and connection." Or the real, long-term deal. Oxytocin is thought to be plentiful in long-term couples with warm, comfortable relationships. It turns out it's released, for starters, "when we hug our children or our long-term spouses" or breast feed our babies.

Maybe that's why, in the wake of my divorce, I've told friends that while yes it might be lovely to fall in love again, what I really want is to have been married for 10 years!

Anyway, back to the "falling in love" part, since we are talking about Valentine's Day. Guys, here's a tip from the piece: If you do something exhilarating and physical on the first date (sorry I'm not talking about sex here) chemicals are released that produce something like that dopamine attachment, and are more likely to get you a second and third date. In other words, take her to an amusement park, not dinner, the first time out.

And keep working at it. It seems women are not the ones more easily swept away by romance, chemically induced or otherwise, after all. We seem to be a little more likely to think in terms of making a choice to love. One study I read long ago showed that men typically fall in love in about three dates, but for women it takes 20.

Happy Valentine's Day.

"Soul Mates"? Schmoul Mates! Looking for Love in all the Wrong Places

January 12, 2012

I wonder if we need to start experiencing marriage more like we experience life with our children.

That occurred to me as I read "You Never Marry the Right Person," the provocative essay by pastor-theologian Timothy Keller. With his wife Kathy, he's the author of *The Meaning of Marriage*, from which the recent piece in relevantmagazine.com is excerpted. Keller writes:

"Today (in marriage) we are looking for someone who accepts us as we are and fulfills our desires, and this creates an unrealistic set of expectations that frustrates both the searchers and the searched for."

Someone who totally accepts us. Totally fulfills us. For life. That's too often how we define "the right person" in our current culture. While that often happens in the movies, it doesn't in the real world. Hence the title of Keller's piece.

But reality doesn't change the fact that today we live in a "find your soul mate" society. Just consider the ever popular romantic comedies, or how online dating sites like eHarmony. com and ChristianMingle.com are promoted.

It's all about soul mates.

Yet, no matter what we think we are getting into on our wedding day, we don't marry the person of our romantic fantasies. We get flawed sinners instead - just like us - because that's all there is! The good news is, he or she may be "right" for us, but in the sense of being someone who will share our joys but also challenge us and call us out of our selfishness in ways we never expected.

Now consider life with our children. We never get the ones we so looked forward to, either. Those perfect little always-delightful things who respond to us sweetly and love us perfectly into our old age. We get the children who present challenges, and difficulties, and outright sin to be dealt with in ways we never thought possible. But who give us joy and enrich us in ways we never conceived of, either. Not least of all because suddenly it's not all about us anymore.

What always amazes me? When I imagined my perfect children, I never foresaw loving them as passionately and wholly as I love the real ones. I couldn't have. That could only come with investing my life and emotions into the real thing.

And by the way we parents usually give more, do more for and love our kids more than what we will receive back from them. But what rightly oriented parent resents that? There is typically joy in such (often exhausting) giving. So, let's pause for a moment and consider how having that orientation toward our spouses might change our marriages!

Yes, there are broken parent-child relationships that are never mended. Tragically, some parents do leave their children. But in general, I've never heard a parent of grown children say, "Wow, that was easy!" But I've often heard, "that was harder, more worthwhile, more meaningful, more heartbreaking, but with moments of more joy than I ever thought possible."

Patiently bearing with each other, sometimes impatiently bearing with each other, with all of our flaws and imperfections brings my children and me to a depth of relationship I couldn't have had with perfect kids. And they couldn't have had with a perfect mom.

Sure, the metaphor only goes so far. For starters, outside of arranged marriages we get a lot more say in our choice of life partner than in our children. But imagine if we thought of our marriages with the same sense of purpose, self-sacrifice, commitment and openness to the unexpected that we typically do our relationships with our kids. We might then find a whole new - only this time real - kind of soul mate in a spouse.

David Cassidy, Teens, and Lessons on Love

February 3, 2011

Valentine's Day is just around the corner. I myself will be celebrating February 14 by going to a David Cassidy concert (seriously, I couldn't resist!) with my almost-12-year-old daughter, Madi.

But this isn't about anything to do with my romantic life. It's about how I'm encouraging my children to look at romance - on Valentine's Day and every day.

My kids are now 16, 14, 11 and 9. And I still believe what I've been saying for years: I don't want them in serious dating relationships when they are not in a position to get married. My view? Date a lot when marriage is at least an option. In the meantime, enjoy lots of friends of the opposite sex, go to dances, have fun, socialize in groups. But pairing off into exclusive romantic relationships as young teens? No, thanks.

Naturally, my children find my view completely at odds with civilization in general. I'm even at odds with many folks who are like-minded with me on other things. My older children in particular are trying to convince me to change my thinking.

But I keep saying what I've always said, romantic relationships are wonderful things designed by God. But He also designed us, and we're designed to want the whole deal, the intimacy, exclusivity and (what should be) the permanence of marriage. It seems to me a romantic relationship stops short of God's design when it can't result in marriage in a reasonable time frame. I.e., an intense high school romance.

Yes, we all know the rare high school sweethearts who went on to a long-term marriage. But it's unusual that real good comes out of exclusive romantic teen relationships. Rather than really learn about the other gender in all facets kids in such relationships are learning about the opposite sex primarily within the confined roles of romantic or sexual partners. That seems too narrow to me.

They also typically learn a lot about breaking up - better practice for divorce than marriage. And the sexual tension (whatever any actual activity), the emotional distress, it's all so intense. How can 15- or 16-year-olds possibly be expected to wisely handle what many adults can't?

Tempted to disagree? Consider this: I've never known a responsible parent who said anything along the lines of "I so hope my children will fall madly in love with someone in high school!" No reasonable parents want that for their child. So why do we fall in line so easily with the culture that seems to demand it?

Far from being a prude, I'm very open and comfortable talking about the wonder of romantic relationships and sex itself with my kids. I just don't want them to settle for too little in such things.

I myself was madly in love by the time I was 15, which they know. But I had no grounding to think clearly about that relationship. I'm not trying to protect my kids from my mistakes.

I am trying to give them a wise grid that I didn't have then to think about dating and love.

And yes, I know I can't control my children. As I've told them, "Look, ultimately you can go against me on this, whether openly or secretly. I can't control you, I don't even want to. I do want to give you a way to thoughtfully consider such things."

In some ways, I'd love for my kids to convince me to change my mind, as it's hard standing against civilization on this one. But I don't expect them to.

In the meantime, I'm happy to be celebrating Valentine's Day with Madi. A "tween" volunteering to accompany her mom to a David Cassidy concert? Now, that's true love.

Divorce – A Personal Report
(and a Little Advice) from the Trenches

June 30, 2011

Another anniversary of mine has just come and gone. I completely forgot this one until I noticed the date a week later. Sort of interesting in its own way, at least to me. It's the anniversary of my then-husband "choosing to go in a different direction," as I sometimes put it, in June 2004.

Well, no big lessons about divorce in this column. I've spoken to those things many times or at least tried to. Rather, this is about the backstory. A little advice, a few points to ponder about the odds and ends of divorce, including some things to think about beforehand. When I share these observations with friends, I often hear in response: "No one talks about that!" So, for what it's worth:

   ✢ Perhaps especially if there are children and the choice to divorce was one-sided, you think at the time you will never be able to deal with your ex without some level of emotional reactivity. And then, almost suddenly, you will likely come to feel an indifference toward him (or her) that's surprising to you. Guess what? The indifference can be kind of sad.

✢ I have shared this with women contemplating leaving their husbands: "For one thing, if you do this he's going to bring women into your children's lives and you will have no control over that." They look at me like I have two heads until they come back a year later in tears because of the woman, and sometimes her children, the ex has brought into their children's lives.

✢ When a husband leaves a wife and children, he withdraws his protection from his family, leaving them vulnerable to a world of men. Not just lousy ones, but good ones who are still capable of breaking the hearts of moms and kids alike. All over again.

✢ If your ex is at all faithful about child support, say, "thank you." It goes a long, long way. Let your children know that you appreciate it, too. As my mother used to say, "You win more flies with honey than vinegar."

✢ If a fellow feels trapped having to support a wife and children while married, he'll really resent it when he has to do it by court order and isn't even living with them.

✢ If you can't influence a spouse much while living together, he or she is not going to suddenly be more open to suggestion from a different household.

✢ No matter what or who ended the marriage, "he was a great skier" or "she was really funny" likely remains true. Find ways to honestly praise your ex to your kids.

✢ If you were faithful to your marriage and didn't want it to end, then don't take responsibility for ending it. It was your spouse's calling to be committed to you even when it was hard. Isn't that what you did for him or her? It takes two to make a marriage work, but one can end it by unilaterally leaving it. Learn from your mistakes in your marriage, sure. But remember that people in life long marriages make mistakes too. It's just that they are rightly given the freedom to fail by their spouse.

✢ Most people won't get the stress and loneliness of being a single parent. Of course they don't. But they themselves have problems and stresses you don't know anything about! Get over yourself.

✢ Find ways to help others in a similar situation, but perhaps behind you a little on the road. That may be the best therapy. Ever.

✢ I see firsthand, and more than ever, that divorce is like tossing a pebble into a pond. You can't imagine where the destructive rings are going to go. It's breathtaking. Whether it's one or both of you contemplating divorce, please think about that before ending a marriage.

I also see firsthand and more than ever how much growth, how much good, can come out of even something as destructive as divorce when God is at work in the middle of it. I keep saying it because I know it's true: His mercies really are new every morning!

The Dangers of Romantic Pornography

October 22, 2009

The recent outrage over the super-skinny Ralph Lauren model caught my attention. You know, the model whose photo was altered in an ad so much that her waist was as skinny as her neck.

The whole thing caused an uproar for creating false standards of beauty among young women, encouraging eating disorders. Frankly, I thought it was all a little over the top. Today's young women in the Western world are far more at risk from obesity than anorexia.

I'm much more concerned about the damage done by false images of women in pornography. There the widespread and easily available portrayal of women as physically perfect and sexually adventurous on a man's terms can create false expectations for a man. And so damage his relationships with real, multidimensional women.

Ironically, I think we hear less about that in a year than we did about the Ralph Lauren model for the several days she was in the news.

But what we hear about least of all is what I now call "romantic pornography" - false romantic portrayals of men in the popular media that no man can really live up to, and which may be so damaging to women's expectations of men and relationships.

I first wrote about this phenomenon years ago when the movie *Titanic* was released. The aristocratic heroine ditches her fiancé because she "falls in love" with the poor but perfect man of her dreams. He captures her heart in a few days, just before he dies a cold watery death. But she loves him forever.

Titanic had young girls swooning about "true love." Ridiculous. One can pretty easily imagine what might have happened if that relationship had hit the real world instead of an iceberg.

Hollywood has turned out a bonanza of romantic-comedy chick flicks in particular in recent years, and it's always the same:

1. Some level of confusion or complication between fabulous romantic man and woman knowingly or otherwise desperately looking for love. Note man's fabulous sensitivity may not be obvious until just the right woman reveals it.

2. Fabulous man finally realizes he cannot live without said woman, and pursues her in a romantic, ever-so-sensitive but oh-so-manly way. Voila! It's happily ever after.

Hey, I can enjoy such chick flicks as much as the next girl. But these are different from the romantic movies of old, where the leading characters of both genders were typically more multi-dimensional. Now, whether it's *Enchanted, The Proposal, Confessions of a Shopaholic, He's Just Not That Into You,* or one of so many others, they are routinely delightful, unrealistic romantic pornography.

I'm far more concerned about my daughters being misled by these portrayals of what men "should" be - and the consistent portrayals of one-dimensional women as romance chasers - than I am by the artificial super-slim models.

Sure, I love romantic gestures like receiving a bouquet of flowers. What woman doesn't? But real romance is loving another over the long term, especially when it's difficult. And in marriage, it is maintaining the commitment even when we might not feel like it in the moment.

So I want my three young daughters to someday judge a man by his strength of character and commitment to them in the ups and downs of real life. Even if he doesn't wear his feelings on his sleeve, or always understand hers.

In other words, I hope I'm raising my daughters in such a way that they don't pass up a real life prince of a man because they are foolishly waiting for today's one-dimensional movie version.

Time to Value a Different Kind of Valentine?

February 11, 2010

Love is all around us or at least, for so many women, it had better be come February 14. Let's face it - Valentine's Day strikes fear into the hearts of guys everywhere because it's so often about getting it right for us gals. Or else!

The origins of St. Valentine's Day are shrouded in legend. My favorite is that Valentine was a third-century Roman priest. Supposedly, Emperor Claudius II outlawed marriage for young men, wanting them to focus on being valiant soldiers instead. The ultimate romantic, Valentine continued to perform marriages in secret. Talk about being willing to die for love. He did - the story goes that Claudius had him executed.

But whatever the outsized legends behind it, little compares with the oversized expectations for romance that Valentine's Day produces in modern times.

According to the National Greeting Card Association, some one billion Valentine's Day cards will be bought again this year. About 85 percent of them will be bought by - you guessed it - gals. I know, I know, women buy most greeting cards. But for a couple's holiday, this seems particularly lopsided.

Anyway, I admit it. I am something of a Valentine's Day rebel. At least as it currently exists. It seems so contrived. And more than a little shallow. Producing cards and flowers and candy on an appointed day is pretty easy.

What about where Cupid meets the ultimate road test of love? Today there's so much fanfare surrounding romantic love, and so little regarding the ultimate declaration of true love in the commitment of marriage. I suppose it's no accident that modern couples often go to increasing extremes to put on elaborate weddings. Often, it seems, without putting anywhere near that same amount of effort into their marriage itself. Call me a cynic, but I wouldn't be surprised if there were a significant correlation between the amount of hoopla that surrounds the nuptials and the couple's likelihood of divorce.

I'm a little more like a dear friend of mine. Married 20 years with several children, she says her husband has probably told her no more than 20 times during all that time that he loves her. They don't even notice Valentine's Day. She doesn't care. He works hard to provide for his family, and is actively engaged in their couple and family life. As she puts it: "He shows me every day that he loves me by being committed to this family and me."

She recently told him that she felt she hit the lottery when she married him. He loved it.

Forget Valentine's Day. That's romance.

But in general our culture will praise the boyfriend who goes to extreme measures for the perfect Valentine's Day celebration more than it will praise the long-term faithful and engaged husband and dad.

We've twisted priorities.

Look, if people want to make a big show of things on February 14, be my guest. For some women and yes, a few guys, that's significant to them. I just think we'd be wise to focus most on the big picture.

Sure, I love being courted. But my own definition of romance in a relationship is to know, over time, that there is a growing connection between us and a deep and abiding care for each other as we consider marriage. In marriage, it would be to know that we are committed for life.

That's true love.

I know, I know: We're only talking one day here. Why not just go with the cupids and the chocolate, and lighten up. Maybe I am a rebel without a cause. It's just that for me, I don't engage in Valentine's Day frenzy because when it comes to romance, I value substance over style.

Why a Remake of Roman Holiday (*and* Casablanca) *Would Sadly Have Happier Endings Today*

April 27, 2006

The other night my family and I watched the classic movie *Roman Holiday*, featuring the most astonishing film actress of all time, or so I'm convinced, Audrey Hepburn. The male lead is Gregory Peck and Eddie Albert is in a supporting role. (Remember him? "Green Acres is the Place to be ... ")

Anyway, this was the film that garnered 10 academy award nominations, brought Audrey fully into our lives, and gave her a Best Actress Oscar.

I suppose everyone knows the story by now: A rebellious and beautiful young princess visiting Rome slips away from her handlers for 24 hours, meets American reporter Gregory Peck - who finally catches on to who she is but pretends ignorance for his own ends - and has a full day of fun and adventure entirely unbefitting a princess.

Eddie Albert serves as the erstwhile photographer secretly chronicling it all, cigarettes, champagne, police station, motorcycle ride, dance party brawl, you name it.

As I marveled once again at the film, as I do every Audrey movie, I wondered if this story could be made today. Not because so many of its themes aren't relevant - think Princess

Di - but because I fear the ending just would not be satisfying to Hollywood decision makers or America's elite.

The movie is 53 years old, so I'm not giving anything away: Audrey, "Princess Ann," hears through the radio about the despair her absence is causing her country people, and she finally decides to return to her royal life and her responsibilities. Gregory Peck, "Joe Bradley," and his counterpart decide not to reveal the princess's escapades, giving up scads of cash they could have made by doing so.

Why? Because Joe and the Princess fall in love, of course. (Yes, I know, only in the movies.) And yet they both decide to do the right thing, which also means they can never have each other. The Princess loved being an ordinary person in Rome for a day, but now she must do her duty and return to her people. In fact, a newly confident Princess Ann makes clear to her close circle of courtiers that duty is the reason she has returned. It's not all about her, or her feelings, or her supposed happiness - it's responsibility to others. And that means she can't apparently have a relationship with an American newspaperman. Nor can we envision Gregory Peck living as the Princess's Consort in some exotic country, anyway.

He forgoes the money and fame revealing her follies would bring him because he also decides to do what is right. Moreover, he knows he cannot have the woman he loves, and he accepts that with all the pain it brings. It's not all about him in the end, either.

We may argue with the social dictates of the day as presented in the film. But the point is that the characters at issue here were called to a sense of duty and they answered that call, even at the cost of their own happiness with each other. Most important, the characters are portrayed in the movie as noble for doing so. Their brief love affair remains a secret.

In early 1950s America, that sensibility made sense. Even to Hollywood. And so the ending was satisfying. The same was true, of course, for the war time classic *Casablanca*.

I just don't know if that would be the case today. Wouldn't there almost certainly have to be a way for the princess and the pauper, as it were, to spend their lives together no matter if it devastated the lives of others? I mean it's all about what THEY want, right?

There are movies made today where there is sacrifice, think *Armageddon*. Of course, there they were all going to blow-up anyway if one didn't sacrifice for the many. But a film where a quiet sense of duty, of calling, of responsibility keeps lovers apart forever and we're supposed to feel that that is noble and right and good, even if sad? I don't think so.

After all, even in the blockbuster tearjerker *Titanic* the star-crossed lovers got together in eternity.

It seems to me that quiet self-sacrifice is still the common lot and pursuit of so many noble Americans, it's just no longer honored in our elite culture. Pursuing our own happiness, even at the expense of others, is.

So, I hope I'm wrong but I just have to think that a remake of *Roman Holiday* would sadly be rewritten today to give us the happier "all about me" ending our culture craves.

Love Potion Number 9 – It May be All About the Dopamine

February 12, 2009

"When the moon hits your eye like a big pizza pie, that's amore. . . "so goes the classic ballad. But, when the dopamine hits the brain? Well apparently that's when things really get crazy. I first wrote about this, and new research on the brain science behind it, back in 2006.

I've always liked what Neely Tucker wrote in the Washington Post from that same year:

"It's all about dopamine, baby, this One Great True Love, this passionate thing (for which) we'd burn down the house and blow up the car and drive from Houston to Orlando just to taste on the tip of the tongue.

"You crave it because your brain tells you to. Because if a wet kiss on the suprasternal notch - while, say, your lover has you pinned against a wall in the corner of a dance club - doesn't fire up the ventral tegmentum in the Motel 6 of your mind, well, he's not going to send you roses tomorrow.

"Dopamine. God's little neurotransmitter. Better known by its street name, romantic love."

Helen Fisher is an internationally renowned anthropologist and an expert on the science and chemistry of, well, love. Her latest book *Why Him, Why Her?* is out just in time for Valentine's Day. I spoke with her recently.

Fisher clarified for me the chemistry connection a little further:

When she studied MRIs of people newly in romantic passion she found that the effect of dopamine on the brain is similar to the rush we would get from . . . cocaine.

Now, says Fisher, her latest research - which has been in part both gleaned from and used in her position as a consultant for the dating website chemistry.com - shows there are four basic personality types, each with its own chemical markers, and they have a lot to do with whom we love. The Builder is calm, persistent, loyal and traditional while Explorers are curious, creative, adventurous, impulsive and self-reliant. Directors are analytical, focused, tough-minded, emotionally contained while Negotiators are imaginative, creative, intuitive, sympathetic and idealistic.

Fisher says we may have traits from across the four basic groups. But most of us tend to be dominant in one, often with a "minor" in another. (By Fisher's lights, I'm definitely a Builder/Explorer.)

So, who is attracted to whom? Fisher says she's found that Explorers tend to be attracted to Explorers and Builders to Builders. But Negotiators and Directors tend to be attracted to each other. Anyway, what makes one attracted to one particular person, or none, out of a room of likely connections? Who really knows? I do believe that thankfully, sometimes even chemistry is a mystery.

And sometimes we miss its most obvious lessons. There was no real news, I suppose, in what Lauren Slater wrote in

National Geographic a few years ago about Fisher's then-new findings, "In the right proportions, dopamine creates intense energy, exhilaration, focused attention, and motivation to win rewards. . . . Love makes you bold, makes you bright, makes you run real risks, which you sometimes survive, and sometimes you don't."

Okay, but what about when the "high" fades, which it almost has to if we are going to live productive (and sane) lives?

Well, there might be news in this: As Slater put it, brain studies from around the world show that almost always the dopamine high of romantic love eventually fades as the brain learns to tolerate it, just like it might increased doses of cocaine. The good news is that in long-term couples, the dopamine eventually gets replaced by oxytocin, a bonding chemical. (The same chemical released when we hug our kids.)

The bad news is when people in a marriage leave a potentially deep, life-long oxytocin connection in order to find another temporary dopamine high. Or, when one jumps through a series of dopamine highs and never experiences an oxytocin connection.

Yes, the dopamine high is magically fantastic. But we are a culture that too often forgets that true love comes in many different, and yet very wonderful, flavors.

Now that's amore.

Chapter Two

What Ever Happened to Courtship?

*When a man loves a woman, can't keep his mind on nothin'
else; He'll trade the world for the good thing he's found.*

- Percy Sledge

In the columns that follow, I don't believe I negate anything
I've said about romance. Pursuit by a man won't necessarily
be about flowers or love songs, or even involve him sharing a
lot of feelings. But it will be clear. There's little doubt that's
how men are designed to operate, and that is typically how
we women want it. If you don't believe me, well, just ask ten
married couples to tell you the story of how they met. A little
more on that follows.

I have often heard the agony of women who are just not sure their guy is into them. A few times I've been that woman. But I now know firsthand, having been wonderfully loved by my fiancé Tom, that what I've long believed to be true *is* true: when a man loves a woman he will naturally court her and pursue her and she won't have to doubt it. A good man wants his beloved to know that she is secure in his intentions of marriage for her. He will be generous to her, and this is not necessarily about money at all. He will want to make her happy. He will be delighted to be her suitor.

I think that's the definition of manly.

I also think that any woman who has to ask, "does he want me?" already has her answer. What she does with that answer, well — I've written some columns that speak to that too.

In these essays I share a little about my own romantic life and choices. I've definitely gone about things in a way that has been at times countercultural, at least by today's standards, and I think you will see what I mean. It's a strange thing to be in the dating world with children. It adds a whole new and central parameter to every choice, at least I think it should. And I know so many single parents can relate to that, too.

So I'll share this: When I was newly a single mom, a dear friend encouraged me to be thankful for my children as I entered the dating world a second time. Why? Because, she said, they would be a sifter for, not a barrier to, a good man. She was so right. Tom pursued me *and* my children. Here are a few of countless examples: Before a recent trip I took with them to Orlando, he gave each a Pez dispenser in the form of a Disney character, with a $20 bill inside and a personalized Bible verse to consider. (And Pez candies, too, of course!)

But it's not just the fun stuff. This renowned scientist was perfectly happy, for instance, to spend hours one Sunday afternoon getting my teenage daughter ready for her high school chemistry final.

This is more than just about the many such gestures he makes. Tom has made it clear he's "all in," and that includes my children. He has delighted in building relationships with them. Now that's pursuit. If you are a single parent, your children deserve nothing less from the one you love.

If He Wants You He'll Pursue You

May 4, 2006

When I was a teenager, my mother gave me one piece of advice on how to handle the world of dating and relationships then opening up to me:

"Don't ever call boys," she said.

Understood was, "the worthy ones will call you."

I'm not sure I thought much of that advice at the time, but lo and behold, decades later as we head toward June and the month for weddings, I've found my mother's wisdom distilled into a new book, *The List: 7 Ways to Tell if He's Going to Marry You - in 30 Days or Less!* by sisters Mary Corbett and Sheila Corbett Kihne.

The List reminds me of the *The Rules*, the 1995 blockbuster book which purported to tell a woman how to get a man to marry her. *The List* tells a woman whether or not he will marry her - and encourages a gal to move on if he's not in the game for keeps.

Yes there are "Rules Girls," but this book is about "List Men."

The List doesn't include much research - just lots of anecdotal case studies - but it sounds like common sense. Try this exercise: For every 10 married couples you know, if you ask "how did you fall in love?" probably nine of those couples will have a story about how he wooed her, pursued her, worked to win her over, etc. Sure, as my mother would say of my dad, she "let him chase her until she caught him," but most happily married couples will have a story of him going after her.

Our feminist sisters may tell us it's just fine to "make the first move/pursue him/sleep with him" you name it. But *The List* makes the case, through all sorts of stories that end up reading like a chick-lit romp, that that's not fine if a woman wants a husband. Or at least a husband worth having.

Here's the bottom line, according to the Corbett sisters. A List Man:

Makes the first move;

Calls within 24 to 48 hours to set up the first date;

Makes the first date easy and fun (and yes he picks up the check);

Calls within 24 hours to set up the next date;

Wants to talk to you every day and wants to spend his free time with you;

Demonstrates unconditional loyalty;

Talks about marrying you in concrete terms and actually proposes, or lets you know his intentions.

The Corbett sisters maintain that if he's "heard the alarm" - meaning "I saw her, I was ready, and that was it" - these things will happen in the first 30 days.

If these things don't happen, they say, then *He's Just Not That Into You*, as one entertaining and best-selling book is titled. Don't take it personally. Just move on.

(*The List* authors suggest every woman who wants to be married make a list of her must-haves for a man. I suggest that list be short.)

Oh, and the Corbett sisters say that if he is into you, if he does hear the alarm, it won't matter what your baggage is for there will be little you can do to dissuade him. In other words, even if one is, say, oh, 43 and suddenly divorced and raising four young kids on her own, just as an example, even that's not going to faze a List Man. Having tested the waters a little bit in that regard, I can say that no one is more surprised than I to find out that the authors may just be onto something there.

I suppose sometimes the question may be determining whether one wants a List Man at all, and just how does one know it's the right List Man, at the right time, anyway? Some questions remain unanswered.

I can say that in my own last few roller coaster and unexpected years, I've decided that this crazy and amazing world is a lot more unpredictable, wonderful, complicated, heart rending and beautiful than I had originally realized. Whether or not I've learned anything about men in particular, I think I've learned a little about people in general.

So taking all that into account, what's the advice I will offer to my girls, and my son, when they one day embark on these amazing things we call relationships ?

Well, I've come up with this little nugget of wisdom: Girls shouldn't call boys. The worthy ones will call her.

It just seems I've heard that somewhere before.

How "I Am Woman Hear Me Roar" Hurts Real Women

You've probably seen the Citi credit card commercial which has generated a lot of buzz. It opens with a woman's voice saying, "My boyfriend and I were going on vacation." She appears to be in a clothing store and needs to get a few accessories. With her Citi card of course. Then the scene changes. She picks out "a new belt" (it's a rock climbing harness), "some nylons" (rock climbing ropes), "and what girl wouldn't need new shoes?" she asks. (Yes, for rock climbing of course.)

Then we watch as she hoists herself up to the tiny top of a huge rock formation we can't believe is real, with the boyfriend following, natch. As we get dizzy watching her triumphantly stand on the little precipice, we hear her in voiceover again: "We talked about getting a diamond. But with all the 'thank you' points I've been earning, I flew us to the rock I really had in mind." In the background we hear the lyrics, "Somebody left the gate open. . . " chime in. (From *Into the Wild* by LP.)

The ad has generated buzz with many folks not believing what they are seeing. But, it turns out the actors are real rock climbers, climbing a real rock formation near Moab, Utah. It's all very glorious.

I can't stand the ad. The narrative drives me to want to climb something!

This is a tough girl who eschews those silly feminine trappings of fashion for real power - high heels for high rocks, and that rock on the third finger of the left hand? Who needs it? Especially when she has all those handy dandy thank you points instead.

Well let me offer this: Her Citi thank you points are not going to keep her warm at night. And they are not going to help her with the baby if she gets pregnant by the boyfriend she doesn't think she needs to marry. Or rather, who doesn't think he needs to marry her. So what's to keep him from finding a younger more attractive rock climber?

And "Somebody left the gate open. .. "? I guess the gate was closed when a rock meant marriage, not hiking.

I know, it's just an ad. But it reflects a culture in which girls are more and more "supposed" to be tough, independent, aggressively sexual and with no need for men or marriage. In fact, that's all seen as constraining in some way.

"I flew us to the rock I really had in mind." Real women create their own destiny, with their own money, and they don't need to consult anyone. Not even someone they might condescend to love.

I am woman hear me roar.

Few real women actually think like this of course. They don't want to man-up themselves, they want the men they love to man-up. And whatever we want in our professional lives, most women want marriage, and children, and a man who will pursue them and in some tangible way care for them. That's how we are built.

That's why this ad, and the culture it represents, is so pathetic. It's not that it depicts reality. It's that it's depicting a "reality" that isn't real at all, but which our culture is apparently trying to create.

Sadly, women aren't empowered by this attempt at social engineering. Marriage rates are plummeting, newspaper articles and books ask, "where have all the good men gone?" and today a majority of babies born to women under thirty are being born to single moms. That means a high probability of poor social outcomes for those kids, as well as much higher poverty and depression rates for those single moms as compared to their married sisters. And that's just for starters.

Yes, I want my own daughters to rise to the tops of their professions. If they want to get to the top of precarious rock formations too, that's great - I hope they tell me about it after they are safely back down.

But you can bet I'm also clear that most real life women want men, and marriage, and family. And so my daughters had better be darn tough. Because increasingly in our culture, it takes a strong woman to admit just that.

Dating After Divorce: Some Different Rules for this Single Mom

October 19, 2006

I think our culture is demonstrably screwed up in how it looks at almost every aspect of divorce.

But here I'll skip over the lead-up, and go straight to taking on the universal belief about dating after divorce: A new relationship shouldn't be introduced to children until it's really "serious." Check out all the divorce books, magazines and online advice, this one is written in stone.

A divorced mom myself, I'm raising my four young kids on my own. But fortunately I have very wise friends who have helped me to see that once again the "experts" here just don't make sense.

Most of the advice is directed at women, because we typically have the children living with us. The universal fear is that children will get attached to a new friend in Mom's life, and then that new friend will be gone.

Can't have that, the thinking goes.

Why not? As long as Mom is thoughtfully dating good and worthy men and is not being sexually intimate with them - major conditions here, for sure - what's the problem? Kids have great adults going in and out of their lives all the time. Teachers for a year, a pastor who takes a call to another church, the Boy

Scout leader who retires, friends of their parents who move away. These can all be great people with whom our children have positive experiences, even though it's for a short time.

That is, well, life. It's the very nature of friendship. It brings joys and sometimes sorrows, but if the relationships are good ones they can enrich us.

Instead, the experts would seemingly have Mom lying to her children and sneaking off to meet some fellow (not exactly great role modeling for when our own kids are teens), only to have the fellow suddenly presented when it's serious. Oh, so Mom, you haven't been out with your gal friends all this time? Great.

Mystery is a scary hardship for our kids, and children of divorce go through too much hardship as it is.

And there's little chance a relationship could become legitimately serious anyway without the fellow having a darn good idea of what his life would be like with a woman's children. Sheesh.

How much better if we single parents set the stage for a healthy dating life for our own children down the road. With a little experience in the matter now, and the wisdom of good friends, here's what makes sense to me and, well, how I've handled it:

Once the divorce was final, I gathered my children and said, "I loved being married, I loved your dad and I'd like to get married again. To that end, I hope to start dating good men. You'll get to meet and enjoy a fellow if we go out a few times and I want to keep seeing him. But think of any fellow as a friend only, unless and until I let you know a special one will become a husband to me and a step-dad to you."

I think it's good for my kids to see me being so positive about men and marriage.

And I know they so appreciate the transparency. Sure, they have different views of me marrying again. While one would prefer to keep me all to herself forever, another actively recruits prospects.

But in any case, I think my openness helps to minimize their fears.

I've had a casual relationship or two now. (Nothing long term, I don't draw things out.) Which means the kids have met a couple of good guys. And when I have, so far, had to end the relationships, I've given my kids some appropriate insight as to why, which I hope will help them to think about how to choose a life partner themselves some day. Even better, if I am eventually blessed with a life partner myself, they will have seen a good process at work. Even if at times it's a bit messy.

Look, I'm not saying my kids have to know everything about my life, or that I always get it right here by any means! I'm certainly not suggesting that there *should* be a series of relationships, I just don't know how to find a marriage partner without going through such steps myself. I am saying that contrary to what the experts advise, I'm not going to deny my children some potentially good experiences, or keep a fellow in the dark about my real life, by sneaking around behind anybody's back here either. That's just no way to start a future.

Time to Take the Online Dating Plunge

January 27, 2011

Time has marched on, and my four children now very much want me to get remarried. I'm in total agreement that that would be a fine thing. In fact, I recently wrote about that in this space.

So now what?

Since my divorce I've dated, of course, and have had chances to remarry, but for various (valid) reasons, declined. So here I sit, sans hubby.

Here's the thing: Last Saturday evening, I made a pretty good spaghetti carbonara dinner, and my older kids and I watched a two-hour special on Adolf Hitler. Really.

Relaxing with my teens on a weekend night? Priceless! OK - I could have been happier with a husband sharing it all. But in order to go out and find said husband, I would have to take time away from things I love doing now, including relaxing with my children, good friends and extended family.

The payoff is great if I find him. But if I don't, I've missed out (and I like to think so have my kids in particular). It's along the lines of ordering a new dish at a favorite restaurant instead of the standard meal you know you love. If it's great, great - but if not, you don't get a good meal at all.

This is a roundabout way of explaining that, with mounting pressure from my children to do so and in hopes of being a little more efficient about things, I'm soon going onto an internet dating site. In the past, I've only dabbled in online dating, in part because I don't want my profile out there for any detractors to find and post. "Hey - here's what that Betsy Hart woman says she wants in a fellow, ha ha!"

I know, I know. Nobody actually cares that much. But come on. I'm a single, middle-aged woman with four children, so please let me flatter myself.

So yes, partly because if I write about it I'll really have to do it and partly because it's just another entry in my "single story" I've been sharing for years anyway, I'll put myself out there ahead of time. Right here.

Here are my non-negotiables for a future husband. He:

- Must be a committed Christian, and if he loves the Reformers, I'll probably fall in love that much faster;

- Must be generous, which has nothing to do with money;

- Must be kind, and someone who will kindly love my kids.

Here's what would be delightful, but not required. I would hope he:

- Is in his early-to-mid 50s;

- Is fit, funny, smart and loves his work;

- ❧ Has friends and won't make me the center of his life, but will love that I make his life better;
- ❧ Is, I admit it, tall. (Well, tallish.)

Here's what I bring to the table:

- ❧ I'm an evangelical Christian who enjoys a vibrant church life and long talks on theology;
- ❧ There's all the superficial stuff that, for better or worse, readers of my column already know about including the fact that I really don't like cooking;
- ❧ Four very cool, very exasperating, very loving kids.

Other basic information:

- ❧ I'll let the right man lead, and I won't ever try to make him my best girlfriend;
- ❧ I'll do all sorts of little things to make him happy because I love doing that for someone I love;
- ❧ I'll support him in his work and his dreams;
- ❧ I'll give him the freedom to fail, and love him anyway.

Of course, I'll hope he's a man who can give me the freedom to fail, and love me anyway, too.

So, I've put it out there. We'll see what it brings. I think this will be fun, while my kids are just thrilled I'm doing *something*. And at least a likely "gentleman caller" can be sure of one thing: My children will be in his corner!

"Suitor" Beats "Boyfriend" for the Marriage Minded

December 29, 2011

Inevitably when the year ends, we are treated to a list of new words that have regularly entered the lexicon in the previous 365 days. This year "Tebowing" - to get down and pray regardless of what others are doing - is new to the language.

Well, at the beginning of 2012, I suggest reintroducing a marvelous and helpful word into usage in the year ahead: Suitor.

A suitor is defined in the World English Dictionary as:

1. A man who courts a woman;

2. A person who brings a suit in a court of law;

3. A person who makes a request or appeal for anything.

All very helpful.

Now, let's make the connection with George Clooney (stay with me here). I fully believe that if women the world over stopped sleeping outside of marriage with the self-declared "I'm never going to get married again" movie star, he would be quick to wed again.

Instead, of course, he gets involved in years-long dating relationships until the woman he is with gets tired of waiting and hoping that she's "different." She realizes she's not. They break up, and he goes on to the next one.

Now, to connect the dots. This same scenario gets repeated in more mundane ways countless times in our culture every day, to the frustration of women everywhere who want to get married. Or, who want to wed in a more timely way than their boyfriends do.

Once, courtship was about finding a marriage partner. Period. In fact, the term "to court" - describing men and women pairing off for marriage - came from the notion of a man "pressing his suit" as he would in court. Making his case to his intended that he would be a good husband.

Now dating, which has replaced courtship, could be about anything. So what's a girl to do when she wants to get married and is not sure about her boyfriend's intentions?

I'd suggest not sleeping with him until marriage and openly declaring "I'm dating to get married," for starters.

But whatever one thinks of such ideas, here's a surefire way to really clarify things: I propose that this be the year for adult, marriage-minded women to ditch the meaningless term "boyfriend." Rather, I suggest resurrecting the old-fashioned term "suitor."

Remember how a man courting a woman is "pressing his suit" for her hand? Perfect. If she starts referring to and introducing her significant other as her "suitor," this will tell her what she needs to know. (She might have to show him an online dictionary, but so be it.)

Is he happy to have friends and family believe he is pursuing her for marriage? Does he embrace the terminology or does he wince at it? Does he want to keep her as his "girlfriend," suggesting the term "suitor" may be a little, you know, strong? Even if he is thinking about marriage, is he put off by the understanding that as the man he ought to be, and we women want him to be, taking the lead in pursuing his beloved?

I'm persuaded that using the term "suitor" can give a girl a lot of useful data in her relationships, very early on. And when, less commonly, the roles are reversed and the fellow isn't sure of her intentions? Try introducing yourself as her suitor, or her as your "intended," and see what happens.

I'm tired of hearing about Clooney's broken-hearted women. I'm tired of the same scenario being repeated endlessly in our culture. I suggest 2012 be the year of the clarifying terminology. Bring back the word "suitor." I'm convinced we would all be better off if it ended up on the end-of -2012 new word list.

And yes, I think the next marriage-minded girl who links up with George Clooney should try using the term "suitor" to describe his relationship to her and see what happens. She will likely save herself a lot of time.

Girls Don't (Shouldn't) Call Boys

March 5, 2009

Ah, if only those poor women had followed my mother's advice. How much better off they would be.

I am of course talking about the girls of ABC's *The Bachelor*. In this week's horrific finale both women finalists who, along with dozens of other women, brazenly threw themselves sexually and otherwise at Jason Mesnick in front of millions of American viewers all season were again humiliated.

Melissa because she was dumped by Jason, also in front of millions of people, after their 6-week engagement. Molly because she was first dumped but then essentially won the final coin toss with Mr. Loyal, who proceeded to make out with her while the sofa was still warm from his dumpee. (Chances of Molly and Jason lasting? Somewhere between zero and none.)

News reports are that millions of women are furious with Mesnick. I say forget the jerk and consider my mother's advice: "Girls don't call boys." Period.

Long before the hit book and film, *He's Just Not That Into You*, my mom had it right: If a man is worthy of you he will pursue you, and only you. If he doesn't, you don't want him anyway.

But times have changed. Any mother of a teenaged son today will tell you about the aggressive girls who pursue their boys. I can tell you about the aggressive single women my age pursuing men. And I'm not talking about subtle hints, charm, and openness to a pursuit. Or even, for a time and if there are some extenuating circumstances, some gentle nudging within a relationship. I'm talking about full bore, desperate, sex-charged male hunting.

It doesn't get much more extreme than several women utterly degrading themselves by sexually pursuing the same man in front of millions of American viewers.

But whatever the scenario, here's why it won't make most men or women happy even if it does occasionally "work" for a time: In the end a man is (gasp!) designed to naturally pursue the woman he loves, and a women to delight in being pursued by the man she loves and can look up to in return.

Not to put too fine a point on it but the reverse is, to varying degrees, pathetic.

Historically it was up to a man to make his suit (as in a court of law) to a woman as to why she should come into his household and under his government and protection, to consider a very old fashioned view of things. This is where the very term "suitor" comes from.

Whatever the modern iteration, it seems to me that if he's not naturally and eagerly making that suit at some level he's not someone a woman would, or should, find attractive. It doesn't mean he's not a good guy, or wouldn't be good for another woman he chose to pursue. It just means that he's not good, or good enough, for her.

Flash forward and the social engineers can say whatever they want to, but here's why we know these instincts remain part of us: Line up 20 married couples and ask how they fell in love and became engaged. 19 of them will have a tale of how he initiated the romance. Mostly you'll hear stories of how he pursued her, risked all for love, etc. She'll often talk about how she wasn't sure at first, but he wore down her resistance. Or, if she was sure, that she "let him chase her until she caught him" as my mom would say about my dad.

Surely the stories aren't entirely true, but even that's a clue as to how we are hardwired to want them to be.

Want more proof? We would cringe to actually hear stories from the wife of her begging and pursuing her husband to marry, sleeping on his doorstep until he said "yes," that kind of thing. Such would be degrading to her. But we love those stories coming from him! It's manly.

So, my three daughters and I watched these women in the humiliating, heartbreaking fright-fest of *The Bachelor* finale.

And at the end of it I looked at them and very simply said, "My dears, a word to the wise: Girls don't call boys."

CHAPTER THREE

A Little Advice (A Lot of Advice) for the Marriage Minded, Newlyweds, and Just About Everyone Else

The best way to succeed in life is to act on the advice we give to others.
- Author Unknown

And just what would be the fun of writing a weekly newspaper column if I couldn't share advice on weddings, as I do in the columns that follow? After all I've hosted one wedding, have attended plenty, and am planning for the second (and last!) time my own. This isn't just about bad manners, i.e., asking guests to wait literally hours between the ceremony and the party while the bridal couple takes pictures. It's about an orientation of self that I have a feeling might be infecting more than a few marriages too.

Particularly when it comes to romantic love today, and certainly marriage, we want to privatize our relationships. But, relationships of any stripe are never just about the two people involved. Because we are human, they always impact a much wider circle than we typically imagine. That's one reason I can't help speaking to the marriage relationship itself here. Not because I got mine all right by any means. But because I was in one long enough, 17 years, to have hopefully learned some things.

And of course as I prepare to marry Tom I have spent a lot of time thinking through, and asking him, how I can be the wife for him he deserves to have.

Yes, in response to a few of these columns I've had husbands in particular let me know they'd "casually" left the newspaper containing my column around the house for their wife to find. That always makes me smile.

Especially since I'm getting ready to marry again, I like to think I'm open to taking my own advice. Of course if not, Tom can always ask me to reread the pages here!

"All About Me" Weddings Are Nothing to Celebrate!

May 24, 2007

The arrival of June means wedding season and that means flowers and elaborate dresses and ... choreographers?

Well yes, Jennifer Saranow writes in *The Wall Street Journal*.

In "The First Dance Spins Out of Control," Saranow recently wrote that ever more young couples, constantly seeking to one-up each other when it comes to what I call "all about me" weddings, are hiring choreographers to stage over the top first dances. Michael Jackson's "Thriller" is a current favorite.

One couple at their recent wedding took places on opposite sides of the dance floor while the DJ got the lights and fog machine ready. Then they went into "the theatrical routine they'd been honing for weeks, performing lifts and turns and pantomiming the sometimes-vulgar lyrics ..."

"We were trying to make it our own little Vegas show," the groom told Saranow.

Ick-eee.

Not to be outdone, another bride required her wedding party's "five groomsmen and bridesmaids to attend four three-hour practices" for their part in the big show. When one of the groomsmen got sick and had to miss a rehearsal, Bridezilla would have none of it. She pulled in one of the understudies she had arranged for from her wedding guests to perform on the big day.

Double ick- eee. (Isn't it enough torture to make the bridesmaids wear those ghastly gowns?)

Another wedding featured a surprise performance from the groom and groomsmen serenading the bride with a choreographed song from *The Little Mermaid* in frog and lobster costumes.

Um, no comment.

Saranow writes that business is booming for wedding choreographers, largely because marrying couples "seem less hesitant to draw attention to themselves by staging dramatic cake entrances, hiring photographers to trail them like paparazzi or posting videos of their elaborate dance routines on YouTube."

Saranow doesn't discuss another "all about me" trend in nuptials, in which it is estimated some 30 percent of couples now stage destination weddings asking friends and family to travel on their own dime to expensive and exotic locales to witness the vows. Maybe they can get a discount for choreography at a destination wedding?

Letitia Baldrige, a manners maven and woman after my own heart, told Saranow that "brides and grooms who make spectacles of themselves on the dance floors show 'a total lack of judgment. ... We're in a culture of show-offs,' " she lamented.

Now I suppose that many folks would argue a couple should be able to show off at their own wedding. But that's the problem - we really do consider weddings and marriages to be all about and only about the two people involved. The growing popularity of Vegas shows at these nuptials may only be a symptom of a larger problem: "All about me" marriages.

Rather, it seems to me a wedding should really honor the couple and their commitment to the larger community and to God. When a marriage is all about me or even all about us, that's a recipe for disaster. Marriage is about connecting to something much bigger than any two people. It's about connecting to the very fabric of a civilized society and understanding it's not all about me. And what a relief that can be!

OK, maybe I'm reading way too much into tacky young people staging elaborate dance productions and other "look at me" trends in weddings. But just in case, I've told my best pals that if I get married again and in a moment of weakness start talking about choreographers or any other such nonsense, they are to stage an immediate intervention on my behalf.

I think some young couples like the ones Saranow describes need better, wiser friends.

Bride and Groom - Now Hear This:
(Your Wedding Guests Will Be Glad You Did)

June 2, 2011

One of my daughters' and my favorite shows to watch together is *Four Weddings* on the TLC channel. It works like this: Four brides attend each other's weddings over a few months, vote on them using a scale of one to 10, and critique them on camera. The highest vote getter among the four goes on a fabulous, all-expenses-paid honeymoon with her new groom. Sure, it gets catty. But it's not all grenade throwing, subtle or otherwise.

Four Weddings is a huge hit. Which made me think, given that June is the traditional season for weddings, why leave so much advice giving to young brides on TLC?

So, yes, here are a few rules of my own I'd like to suggest to engaged couples. Whether your wedding is next weekend or next June, I hope you'll find some things here to consider:

Rule 1 - Start with the guest list. Less is more. By many accounts, the average guest costs the wedding hosts $170. Reason enough to cut the guest list many times over. More to the point, 10 years into our marriage my then-husband and I looked at photos of the 140 folks who were part of our wedding day and realized we had no on-going relationships with at least half of them. And, unless you are throwing a

Donald Trump-level bash, the vast majority of folks you know who aren't very close family or friends will be happy to not be invited anyway.

Rule 2 -Assuming you followed the first rule, your guests are people who love you. They are not just props in your Bridezilla show. So be considerate of your guests in every way possible. For instance, have your wedding and reception in the same place or near each other, even if the venues are not otherwise "perfectly perfect."

And please minimize your guests' awful down time between the wedding and reception. It unnecessarily adds sometimes hours to the whole event - typically boring hours, at that. Consider taking all or most of your photos before the wedding so you can go straight to the party. You'll have more fun that way, too. This means the bride and groom will see each other before the wedding itself, but who cares? Why make that the one tradition you keep? Most of you have been living together before your marriage anyway. Get over yourselves.

Rule 3 - Do whatever your budget will allow, but please do it well. If you want a sit-down dinner, don't try to spread a reasonable budget for 20 to cover 200. Consider a luncheon instead, equally lovely. In my book, it's preferable. (See Rule 1 – "Less is more.") Just be clear to your guests about what you are, and are not, providing in the way of food.

Rule 4 - Leave the party before your guests do. This was once standard. Watch the *Father of the Bride* movies if you don't believe me. If instead you party down with your guests until two in the morning, you make it hard for other folks to leave. And you announce to the world that you've already had so much sex with each other that, frankly, it's no longer anything to rush off for. (Yes, here for the sake of good manners if it's not all new — please pretend it is.)

If you cling to the party until most of your guests have slunk out simply because it's your one big day to be the center of the show, you likely have your priorities messed up. Maybe really messed up.

The fact is you do have something better to get to, the beginning of your marriage! Whatever happens at a wedding I attend, when the bride and groom clearly have that orientation, I can't help but give the whole affair a perfect "10."

Hey Newlyweds, Listen Up! The Wedding is Over Now it's all About The Marriage

April 7, 2011

Discussing what feels like the commonality of divorce in our circles, a dear gal pal whose own son is getting married soon pondered how to prevent marital breakup. She asked for my advice. Yep. She really did. Me. A woman married for 17 years, then blindsided by divorce, and now single for over half a decade. What could I possibly have to offer?

Who cares? I'm up for the challenge! Over the years, I've observed a lot, and learned a lot, and heard a lot, so I'll put a few things out there.

To brides everywhere: At the top of the list for your husband is, likely, sex. Actually, it is the list. Many years ago, I heard a young mom advise a group of wives to "find out how much sex your husband wants. And give him more." Bingo. Still, I'm convinced that too few wives of any age understand how crucially important sex is to their husbands both physically and, yes, emotionally. Well, whether you figure it out or not, just do it. A lot.

Meanwhile, seek to respect and encourage your husband. I suggest resisting the urge to whine, and instead thanking him on a regular basis for working hard to support you, for being a good dad to your kids. Anything that will genuinely build him up. That will go further than you can know in making him eager to please you and care for you.

And please do not attempt to make your husband your best girlfriend. He's not built for that, and you don't really want him to be, anyway. Get a gal pal. Get lots of gal pals. Look to them for much of your emotional support, and you will be happier for it.

Meanwhile, husbands, when it comes to your list (i.e., sex), here's a tip: Helping around the house and being a great, involved dad to your kids may be the ultimate aphrodisiac for your wife. A little seduction will help, too. I have a friend who explained it to her husband this way: "Honey, often I really don't want to get dressed up to go to a party. I have to be talked into it, sometimes cajoled. But I'm always happy when I actually get to the party that I put the effort in to getting there." So guys, instead of being impatient or demanding, how about working a little harder to encourage your wife to want to get dressed for the party? You see?

Fellas, treat her as if she's really special. Even more so after the kids come, because they don't typically say, "Great job, Mom!" Little thinking-of-you gifts, a book, a favorite CD, something she mentioned. Don't worry so much about being romantic. Most wives just want to know that their husbands are listening and that they really care.

And husbands, please forget everything that modern feminism and popular culture have told you as they've pooh-poohed you being a leader in the family, and just do it anyway. Virtually every wife wants to feel protected and cared for by her husband. We really do need you. And we want to know you would slay dragons for us, whether that's a politically correct sentiment or not.

In the end, of course, marriage is ultimately about whether spouses are willing to keep their marriage vows and faithfully love their partners even when the other isn't doing all - or any - of the "right" things. And yes, as previously noted, I'm just a middle-aged formerly married person. But for what it's worth, I'm just sayin': If something can make marriage more satisfying and fun and fulfilling along the way, why not ... just do it?

Wives, Time to Lighten Up on Your Guy?

July 20, 2006

A recent study from University of Virginia research-ers found that whatever our political views, women who are in long-term committed marriages with husbands who are emotionally involved, make most of the money, and help with the household chores in a way that's "fair" report "the highest levels of marital happiness."

Um gee, do ya think? I mean, what else is there?

These days men are supposed to "bring home the bacon, fry it up in a pan ... " and get up in the middle of the night to chase down some unknown noise from somewhere in the house. And that's all while listening to and understanding our deepest feelings and emotions. But is it ever enough for us?

Here's the answer: A dear guy friend of mine told me years ago that his philosophy was, "you can never satisfy a woman - you can only distract her for a short while."

Why is that?

Maybe it's because of what writer John Tierney calls "the complaint gap." Women just ... complain more than men do. (And boy is THAT gutsy for a guy to point out.)

Anyway, there was a lot of great information in the study, published in the March issue of *Social Forces*, a top sociology publication. Sociologists Steven Nock and W. Bradford Wilcox found, for instance, that women want their husband's help around the house in a way that's "fair." But if he's working hard outside the home too, they don't expect him to pitch in 50-50 whatever the feminists might say. That makes sense to me.

My concern is that the researchers found that the number one predictor of marital happiness in the study was the level of emotional engagement of the husband, and so this is interpreted to be a good that he should obviously provide.

Sure, emotional involvement means different things to different people. But another friend of mine (I have wise friends, what can I say?), an older woman, once observed to me that historically, women found that their deepest emotional connections came primarily from other women. That's why women can spend four hours with a group of friends doing almost anything or absolutely nothing and yet at the end of it know EVERYTHING about each other's lives. But men can spend four hours, say, playing golf with their best friends and yet know nothing more about the other fellows at the end of it all other than what they each shot.

Of course women of an earlier day loved their husbands, but the need for deep emotional understanding and sharing was often met by women friends who were similarly built for connection.

Ahh, then the feminists came along, and said "oh no, understanding her deepest feelings and needs was for a woman's mate to do, and if he doesn't - he's a jerk !" And that's when a lot of trouble started.

But what if he's not a jerk, what if he is our best friend and companion but still we recognize that he's just built differently than we are? Why isn't that OK?

I think one of the great things about marriage is that we can learn to appreciate someone so different from ourselves, and learn from the different kinds of strengths our spouses bring to that union. We can and should call the best out of our mates, and sometimes this might include encouraging from them a bit more - or yes, less - response on an emotional level.

I just observe that when it comes to addressing gender issues, more and more there seems to be only one direction in our culture: Women asking, demanding, that men be more like us.

I see that causing problems large and small, in the home and in our society. So yes, I guess I'm being a "girl" - and complaining about it.

What Men Want
(And it's Not JUST What You Think)

August 5, 2010

It's not every day a woman gets to observe a bunch of guys learning how to develop significant relationships with women. But that's exactly what I was allowed to watch a few weeks ago.

The men gathered in a "boot camp" led by Dr. Paul Dobransky. "Dr. Paul" is a practicing psychiatrist in Chicago who has a special interest in relationships and what makes men and women tick. These guys were learning how to approach a woman and understand her signals, what's important to her, how to court her and how to choose the right woman for a long-term commitment.

The boot camp, which Paul and his staff conduct about once month, comes with a price tag: $1,800 apiece. Seriously.

So, these must have been socially inept nerds, right? No. Here's what so surprised me as I met the men in a Chicago restaurant, and listened to them talk: The four gathered for this session were all nice-looking, intelligent, sociable, professional fellows. They ranged in age from late 20s to early 40s.

To paraphrase a lament from the *Sex and the City* girls, "everyone knows a million great single gals - but no one knows a million great single guys." So with the deck so stacked in their favor, why in the world is any guy shelling out big bucks for this class?

Well, here's what the "students" told me: They don't think the deck is stacked in their favor at all. Yes, they agreed, there are lots of single women out there and yes, they are typically sexually available. But, what these guys so want, and what they assured me their (honest) friends also admit to wanting, is to find a woman who really believes in her man. Who respects him, looks up to him, cares about his work and knows how much of his identity he's built to derive from it. A woman who thinks he can do anything. That, they agreed, is so crucial. And so rare.

That was my biggest takeaway, and something Paul says he hears all the time. Yes, his is a self-selecting group, but it makes sense to me. Relationships today are so geared to a woman's needs - is he sensitive, does he understand her, does he take care of the kids and listen to her feelings.

Of course, women should be treated well. But in our dialogue on relationships today, there seems to be very little interest in a man's needs.

I've seen lots of advice in the popular culture, for example, about dealing with the "callous" husband who doesn't do enough housework or childcare even when he works full time and she is home full or part time. But I can't recall the reverse - an instance when such a wife was advised to learn about her husband's work and how important it is to him, and to regularly let him know how much she admires him for laboring so hard to support their family.

I've often whined about this trend, which manifests itself in so many ways. It's what I call the feminization of the culture.

Paul says it also has to do with the way men are built. He notes that, unlike women, it's typically difficult for men to ask for a need to be met, including "I need you to respect and honor me."

So, Paul said it's not surprising that when a man in our culture finds a woman he is attracted to and who admires him as a man, he typically feels he's found a gem. A rare one.

Anyway, after a few hours, I left the guys to continue with their "studies." I newly appreciated that the numbers don't tell the whole story, and that men don't have it so easy after all. No matter how we distill it down, relationships between men and women will always be wonderfully challenging and mysterious.

And, by the way, Paul also teaches classes for women, including skills for discovering that right guy. I think maybe I'll see if I can drop in on that one next time.

For more information, visit www.doctorpaul.net.

For the Sake of the Kids Make
Your Spouse Your Priority

July 24, 2008

"S.G." writes to Carolyn Hax, a nationally syndicated advice columnist, that she's almost 50 years old and
has been dating a wonderful man for three years. Though they
maintain separate households, their lives are otherwise intertwined: Seeing each other all the time, maintaining mutual cal-
endars, joining in each other's family celebrations, kids' events
and so on. They each have three high school/college aged
children. She's ready to get married and officially merge the
households already so connected. He says such a merger would
upset his kids and says "no" for now. S.G. thinks his kids are
conspiring against her.

Hax sides with him. Essentially, Hax says, the kids' feelings
need to come first. She encourages S.G. to wait for marriage
until the kids are all out of the homes.

Whoa.

Okay, Hax. While I've often shared my advice through
opinion, every once in a while I ache to tell it straight. So, nudge
over for a minute, please, while I cut through your befuddled
pop-culture think and speak to S.G. directly.

Dear S.G.:

Betsy here . . . listen up and wake up.

Three years of this? Are you kidding me? How do you know Mr. Wonderful won't also object to a merger if it upsets his kids while they are meeting their own spouses, having their babies, getting their own divorces?

I'll make the safe assumption you are sleeping with him. One way to find out Mr. Wonderful's true intentions? Stop doing so. Right now. And not again until you are married. Period. This isn't (just) a moral issue it's a "girl, get smart!" issue.

Do you want your daughters in long-term relationships where they are giving themselves sexually without the commitment of marriage? Or your sons to be able to live in perpetual adolescence, without having to grow up and make a commitment to the woman they love and are sleeping with?

No? Then you shouldn't live that way either.

Now, you need to sit down with your beau and talk about a few things. Marriage is about far more than the two people involved. It's a covenant that tethers a community and a family. Does he see it that way? Find out, because if it really is only about the two of you, it won't last long anyway.

OK, the kids. Assuming Mr. Wonderful is a man of character and worthy of your children (and other people whose opinion you trust agree), one of the greatest gifts you and your beau could give all of your children would be the gift of living together within a healthy, committed marriage. One which becomes the centerpiece of the home, giving them a security they can't have now if any of them are calling the shots as much as you suspect.

In fact, all the kids need to understand that they don't, or shouldn't, ever occupy a place in your hearts that only a husband or wife can fill. So then, there really isn't any "competition" for them here. I'm not saying it's easy for the children to get this truth, I'm saying it's up to you and your intended to lovingly help them to see it over time.

And by the way, a marriage between you and him will only work if your children see you two being united in dealing with them, for their good. They will try to manipulate you against each other just as kids do their biological parents. Your children will, very soon, grow up and out of the family nest. Your relationship with any new spouse will (we hope) last the rest of your lives. Your first responsibility, for the well being of all of the children as well as your spouse, needs to be to your marriage just as it should be when biological parents are married.

Patience, time, and some really well-grounded counseling for the whole family are musts. Will there be logistics to figure out, and trials to deal with? Of course. But if you give your children the gift of seeing marriage as sacred and worth working through those difficulties (or trying to) for the sake of all of you, you will have given them a gift indeed.

And if Mr. Wonderful doesn't get it then he's not Mr. Wonderful, and you need to stop wasting your time and move on.

Thanks for letting me weigh in - good luck to you, S.G!

CHAPTER FOUR

Why Marriage Matters

*In your love you see only the heaven of your own
happiness, but in marriage you are placed at a post of
responsibility towards the world and mankind.*

-Dietrich Bonhoeffer

Our culture has such a strange view of marriage today. It
means nothing and anything all at the same time. So, why
is marriage important anyway? The columns that follow speak
to all this, and some from a very personal perspective. But
don't take my word for it. Consider just a few conclusions, well

supported by the social science data, on exactly why marriage is so foundational to relationships and to a successful society.

The following is adapted from *Why Marriage Matters: Twenty-Six Conclusions from the Social Sciences*, 2nd edition, 2005, a publication of the Center for Marriage and Families at the Institute for American Values, New York City:

- Marriage increases the likelihood that fathers and mothers have good relationships with their children;

- Cohabitation is not the same as marriage. Cohabiting couples on average are less committed, less faithful, and more likely to break up than married couples;

- In almost every known human society, marriage exists as a way of regulating the reproduction of children, families, and society;

- Marriage typically fosters deeper romantic and parental relationships compared to other family forms, such as cohabitation. Individuals who have a firm commitment to marriage as an ideal are more likely to invest themselves in their marriage, and to enjoy happier marriages;

- Married women have a lower risk of experiencing domestic violence than do cohabiting or dating women;

- A child who is not living with his or her own two married parents is at significantly greater risk for child abuse.

Yes many children from single parent families grow up to be wonderful, healthy adults. Many children with both parents in the home have problems.

But, I don't know any divorced person who says, "I hope my children never marry." Or, "I hope my children marry, then get divorced."

Being or staying married might not always be possible. As a single mom, unwillingly divorced myself, I know this to be true. But that doesn't change the fact that when it comes to healthy relationships and healthy communities, marriage really matters.

Rising Rates of Single Parenthood:
Putting Moms and Kids at Risk

February 23, 2012

Today for the first time in the U.S., a majority of babies born to women under the age of thirty are born to single mothers. That's according to research done by the Washington, D.C. group Child Trends, which it further teased out for *The New York Times*.

After some stabilization in the 1990s, rates of out-of-wedlock births in the U.S. have gone back to skyrocketing. And so headlines over the last several days have screamed exactly that. It's worth screaming about. Children born out of wedlock face obstacles in every area of life when compared to their peers born to married parents. From financial security to emotional well being, the odds are they will have a tougher time. Interestingly, the fastest growth in unmarried births in recent years has been among white women in their twenties with some college education.

The reasons for the staggering rise are hotly debated. But few debate - anymore - that high rates of single parenthood have huge consequences for the children involved.

But what about the women? Maybe it's because I'm a single mother myself that I ask the question. If such a significant percentage of our younger generation are having children without being married at all, and if this has any measurable consequences for them, then this too could impact our culture in significant ways.

So I talked to Dr. Bradford Wilcox, director of the respected National Marriage Project located at the University of Virginia. The Marriage Project provides research and analysis on the state and health of marriage in the U.S.

Unsurprisingly, he told me, the data is clear that single mothers are far more likely to be depressed than married or cohabiting mothers. Now, while some of the recent news reports about the climb in unmarried births point out that most of these babies are born to cohabiting couples, and yes there are similar rates of happiness in the two groups, watch out: Wilcox cautioned that cohabiting couples are twice as likely to break-up by the time a child is five than are married couples.

His point is that single moms who have their first baby with a cohabiting partner are at high risk to be parenting on their own early in their child's life. One of the devastating consequences for these single moms in any event? According to Elizabeth Wildsmith, a research scientist with Child Trends, these moms have a much lower likelihood that they will marry. Ever. (Less research has been done on the correlation for men and marriage after fathering children out of wedlock, though there also appears to be some association.)

Whether that's because of the children themselves or the circumstances and choices that brought a woman to single parenthood to begin with - or all of the above - it's hard to tease out.

But it's important because married women and men are typically, and by large margins, happier and better off financially, physically and emotionally, than their single peers. For starters, "married young adults are between 11 and 28 percentage points more likely to report that they are 'very happy' with life, compared to their unmarried peers. . ." That's just one of a host of findings from "When Baby Makes Three: How Parenthood Makes Life Meaningful and How Marriage Makes Parenthood Bearable," from the Marriage Project's latest *State of Our Unions* annual report, released in December 2011.

Single parenthood has devastating consequences for children. But it also has devastating consequences for the parents. One of the most concerning and clear implications is that single moms are more likely to be shut out from the marriage market and its benefits. Maybe for good.

How tragic that we've moved from a "save women and children first" culture, to one which so easily tolerates women and children being put at risk.

Easy Relationships Offer No Paradise

October 6, 2011

"There are two ways it is easy to do things with other people," my pastor friend recently shared. "If they are exactly like us, or do exactly what we say. Any other situation becomes complicated."

Of course, the statement was made with irony in that Sunday-morning sermon. As my pastor went on to explain, we were actually created to have complex relationships. We were designed to listen to and understand others. To be called out of ourselves. And that was true before The Fall.

He pointed out that that first husband and wife, even in the perfection of Eden, were learning how to "dance through life together without stepping on each other's toes."

I would add that, in a fallen world, we need to learn how to give and receive grace in relationships when we inevitably do step on each other's toes. I thought of all this as I heard a young single friend mention recently that marriage, that most intimate of human relationships, sounds like "work," so why bother?

It seems to me a lot of people, young and old, are asking exactly that. It's likely one reason why marriage rates around the world are plummeting, including in the U.S. Couples are still coupling, of course, they are just increasingly living together without being married. That, in turn, allows a person to walk away from a troubled relationship more easily than one can today walk away from a marriage.

I've written many times about the positive benefits of marriage. But surely one that doesn't get so much appreciation is the work it takes. And I don't mean the kind that is just gutting through things to get to the other side.

Consider that in almost anything in life, we hold most dear what we have invested in the most heavily. What has cost us. Who goes to medical school thinking, "I know it will be a piece of cake, and that will make it worth it"? Does anyone come back from the gym and say, "I didn't work out very hard at all - I feel great"?

We would find such things silly. But, suddenly, when it comes to relationships in general, and marriage in particular, we get scared off by the work involved.

When a man and a woman come together in matrimony, they are starting from a point of being very different. That's a gift! When you strive to serve and understand and appreciate and have patience with someone who is innately so different, your own soul can expand in a way it might never do otherwise.

What an amazing opportunity so many people miss when they live together without marriage so they can easily walk away if things get rough.

It seems we have fewer opportunities than ever for permanent relationships. Marriage aside, members of extended families - in which one could surely experience the gift of complicated, enduring relationships - now often don't live near each other so there's no need to interact much. People often choose to have fewer and, increasingly, no children, perhaps because it's easier that way. And on it goes.

Of course, I'm all for joyful, fun relationships. They can be a taste of heaven. But the conflict and just the complexity of permanent relationships can be a gift too.

Yet in so many ways we can and do avoid the work of relationships today. What's interesting is that I sure don't notice a culture of people happier for it. Maybe it's that without the work of relationships, it's just easier to live selfishly today than it used to be.

I think that is a taste of paradise lost.

Living Together Outside of Marriage? Grow up!

March 11, 2010

I recently attended the lovely wedding of a beautiful young couple. She's 23. He's 27. The festivities were classic and the bride and groom radiant.

But what struck me most is that, statistically speaking, this union has a great chance of lasting for a lifetime, and even a high probability that it will be a happy one.

Unlike many couples who marry today, this bride and groom didn't live together before the wedding.

A new Centers for Disease Control and Prevention report again shows that couples who live together before marriage, especially if they are not engaged at the time they move in together, are more likely to break up after they marry than those who don't cohabit before their wedding day.

It appears the trend is here to stay: More than half of young people today will live with one or more romantic partners before marriage. It's the new normal.

And that's a problem. Weddings like the one I just attended are simply becoming less common. Marriage rates in the United States have fallen considerably as cohabitation rates have risen.

David Popenoe is the former director of The National Marriage Project, now based at the at University of Virginia.

As director, he explained in a report titled *Cohabitation, Marriage and Child Well-Being*:

"The yearly number of marriages per 1,000 unmarried women age 15 and older has dropped by nearly half since 1970, from 76 to 41 in 2005. A major reason for the decline of marriage rates is precisely the rise of cohabitation. Without the possibility of cohabitation, a much higher percentage of the population would be married; (for) there has been little decrease in recent times in the propensity of young people to desire to 'become couples.' "

Now this trend is, in a word, nuts. There is no question that on a macro level communities with higher marriage rates are more stable, affluent, educated and have lower rates of crime. On a micro level, and most importantly, children are more likely to thrive when their biological parents are married. Conversely, the evidence is clear that children are at greater risk of negative social pathologies - especially ending up in a single-parent home - when a parent is living with an unrelated partner or when the biological parents are living together unmarried.

But there's more on the micro level than just the well-being of children. It turns out that married couples are more likely to be happy than those just living together.

According to Popenoe, "cohabiting partners tend to have a weaker sense of couple identity, less willingness to sacrifice for the other and a lower desire to see the relationship go long term." Even in countries where cohabitation has become the norm, studies show that those living together are typically less satisfied with their romantic relationship than are their married friends.

This isn't just self-selection. Decades of research also shows that those who don't cohabit before marriage are more likely to be happy than those couples who marry but lived together before their wedding day.

This makes intuitive sense to Paul Randolph, director of Insight Christian Counseling outside of Philadelphia and a marriage therapist for 25 years.

He told me that he has consistently found in his years of counseling husbands and wives that "couples who lived together before marriage have a higher degree of unresolved conflict on major issues in their marriage compared to couples who didn't live together before marriage. The latter even seem to have happier sex lives."

When it comes to marriage, there are no guarantees. I had all the statistics on my side, too, and I'm divorced. And many couples who live together before the wedding day go on to have happy marriages.

But I know that I loved watching that young couple literally start a new life together. There was something inherently special about the step they were taking. Sadly, it may be an increasingly rare occurrence. Maybe that's one of the reasons this particular wedding was such a cause for celebration.

Falling Marriage Rates: Uh-oh Watch Out Below

October 26, 2006

"**Danger: Watch out for Falling Trend in Married** Households," or so should have read the recent headlines announcing a stunning statistic: The American Community Survey, a report from the U.S. Census Bureau, revealed that for the first time in America's history a *minority* of America's households are now headed by traditionally married couples, with or without children.

While just a few decades ago 75 percent of all households in the Unites States were headed by married couples, that figure has been declining for decades and now stands at just under 50 percent. The rest consist of single heads of households (like yours truly), singles, couples living together without being married, gay couples and so on.

Most adults still want to get married, and most eventually will. Still, the decline in overall marriage rates is important.

That's because the data is clear: The traditional institution of marriage civilizes men, protects women and children, and provides stability to the community. Just because each marriage does not do this is irrelevant to what marriage was designed to do and in fact, typically does.

So the question is, are we at a tipping point yet when it comes to whether or not we as a culture value and sustain marriage? That's a crucial question even for those living outside of marriage. For instance, I am raising my kids on my own but they still derive huge benefits, including safety, community stability, male and family role modeling and more from living in the neighborhood we do in which marriage rates are quite high.

If increasing numbers of children aren't getting that either in their own homes or in their neighborhoods or larger communities, the negative cascading effect might be profound.

So what' going on? Here's one part of the puzzle, another report entitled "Why Men Won't Commit," part of the *State of Our Unions* series from the National Marriage Project at The University of Virginia. (While recently reported at MSN.com, the study is from 2002.)

Anyway, I saw the headline and it was easy to guess the first several reasons. Sure enough the study of younger men, age 25-33, showed that:

- ✝ Men can get sex without marriage more easily than in times past.

Duh.

- ✝ Men can enjoy the benefits of having a wife by cohabiting rather than marrying.

Double duh. (Thanks feminist foremothers.)

- ✝ Men fear that marriage will require too many changes and compromises. (Um yes. It's supposed to.)

- ✝ Men savor their freedom to enjoy late nights out and freedom from extra financial burdens.

Please refer back to "marriage civilizes men."

- Men face few social pressures to marry.

- Men want to enjoy a single life as long as they can.

- Men enjoy the freedom of not having to be responsible to anyone else.

Triple duh?

Dropping marriage rates, and the younger men who seem to be championing that trend (with a whole generation of complicit women, reluctant or otherwise) are perhaps a symptom, not a cause, of a much larger problem our society faces: Think Peter Pan meets It's All About Me. For today we encourage men in particular, but women too, to engage in an extended adolescence instead of marrying.

Ouch. It doesn't bode well for the culture.

Look, I'd love to do my own small part for the declining marriage rates and get married again myself. But one girl can only do so much!

To reverse this trend, our culture as a whole has to value marriage precisely by emphasizing that marriage is not all about me. It's a calling to be about others and that's the place to find real joy and satisfaction, anyway.

But sadly that sure is a tough sell in our current age. And that's why the signs here point to "Danger Ahead!" for our culture.

Who Needs Marriage? I Do!

December 2, 2010

Referring to plummeting marriage rates and chang-ing views toward marriage in the United States, a recent cover of TIME magazine asked: "Who Needs Marriage?"

I could name all the reasons our culture does. But I've written that column more than once. Here, I'll answer the question more personally: I need marriage. Or, at least, very much desire it.

Either way, that's not the politically correct response. I'm supposed to say that, in the wake of my unexpected divorce five years ago, I'm a strong, independent woman wonderfully now "finding myself" and all that. Nonsense. I wasn't lost, so what would I be looking for, anyway?

My situation is a little unusual, I suppose, in that my four school-aged children sleep in my house every night. That's a lot to handle on my own, which means I often don't do it all well.

Wow, would I be happy to have my children hear "Don't talk to your mother like that!" from a loving husband. It would also be great for them and me to have someone regularly help, even just a little, with putting up Christmas lights, getting the car's oil changed, killing spiders, hiring contractors, overseeing homework, yelling about bad grades - and celebrating good ones - and all the other things associated with life.

Come on. It's supposed to take two to successfully parent.

But marriage is certainly not, ultimately, about sharing parenting, which has a limited shelf life. At least, it shouldn't be. It's about sharing a life. As a woman, I want to feel protected and cared for by a husband. I believe I'm - gasp! - built to want that. But it's also about what I'm built to uniquely give to one man committed to me: My support, respect, admiration and encouragement, and all without ever trying to make him my best girlfriend! Without a spouse, right now I'm not able to give full expression to those things.

And yes, I'd love to wake up in the morning with a husband in my bed, instead of various children and animals sacked out in my room. And no, I'm not going to play at being married without being married.

I even need the conflict of marriage. Really. Bearing with a man, with someone so different from me, giving him the freedom to fail and still loving him, would again stretch me as a human being. A lot. Humbly receiving that same forbearance from him? Well, that's part of what I need, too.

This is all very different from being needy, by the way. I'm happy in what I consider a very full, interesting and fun life. And on the flip side, having been married for 17 years I'm quite aware that no man or woman can ultimately meet another's needs anyway.

But I believe that men and women were built to need and want each other, and give to each other, in a unique way in marriage. A way that often allows us to more fully express our humanness.

All that said, I still find I'm at peace with a need I fully recognize because I know that God is (somehow) using it for my good right now. In other words, I don't deaden myself to the good and powerful desire for marriage, as I fear so many today do. I do choose to walk and grow with Him in the midst of the need I admit, that's all.

Maybe that's why I just don't feel defensive, or less than the strong, capable woman I am, when I openly admit that when it comes to "who needs marriage?" The answer is, well, "I do."

The Case for Short Courtships and Marrying Young - Really

September 8, 2011

So my teen and tween daughters are at it again: Pushing me to allow dating relationships for them now, or in the cases of the younger ones, pushing for a promise that I will allow them to have such relationships when they are teens.

I think the advent of the school year has something to do with revisiting the issue. Sigh.

In February of this year, just before Valentine's Day, I wrote about this very thing. How I feel confident that intense, exclusive dating relationships for teens, when they are in no position to marry, are a little crazy. Yes, I realize that pegs me as being slightly insane, at least according to my children. No, I don't think I can fully prevent such relationships even with my own kids. I get it. Eventually, I won't, I can't be their conscience anymore.

But with my oldest daughter being only 15, I still have a lot of conscience duties in their lives. Anyway, what I didn't talk about so much in that piece is what I have long believed in, and it's the flip side of the "I think dating relationships in your teens are nuts." It's that I advocate young marriage (meaning, finishing college at a minimum) or moving any legitimate dating relationship along quickly toward marriage. And if it's not clearly moving in that direction and in a reasonable time frame - end it.

Back to kids. I know parents who know their teens are in an intense dating relationship and assume (often rightly) that they are having sex in some form. But I also see parents, particularly in my evangelical world, who focus on helping teens have chaste romantic relationships for long periods since the young people are in no position to marry. And so there is a lot of focus in this world on "chastity balls" and "purity rings."

In contrast, I think long-term chaste romantic relationships - teen or otherwise - are, well, unnatural.

Sure a lot of Christians, and even Christian parents, will disagree with me. But here's my point: Even where truly chaste romantic relationships are possible over the long term, barring some extenuating circumstances it's not supposed to be that way. Romantic love and sexual love go together. Hello. That is simply how we are designed. We are supposed to combine the two. They are good things and are meant to go together.

In fact, I've come to believe that having a long-term, sexually chaste romantic relationship can be just about as perverted as having a sexual relationship without marriage.

No wonder, as sociologist Mark Regnerus pointed out in his provocative *Christianity Today* piece, "The Case for Early Marriage," almost 80 percent of young adult, conservative, churchgoing Protestants who are dating are engaged in some level of sexual activity. When it comes to young people, where evangelicals have tried to kick it up a notch and promote chastity balls and promise rings, it's for the most part not working. Hello, again. It is not supposed to!

Regnerus says that what we should be doing is better equipping our youth to marry young and have successful marriages. No, not just so that young people can have legitimate sex, but so that they can grow up and live fully. He laments, I think rightly, that even the Christian world increasingly sees marriage not as "a formative institution, but rather as the institution they enter once they think they are fully formed."

Regnerus' research shows that it's not young marriage, per se, that is the problem in many marriage breakups, but rather a lack of preparation for the realities of marriage.

Back to my children. I would love for them to delay serious dating relationships until marriage is an option. Then date a lot, but not any one person for too long, and get married in a reasonable time frame and at a relatively young age. With the understanding, of course, that marriage is about a covenant, it's not "all about me."

I don't know what will happen with my children when it comes to their romantic life, but I do admit this much: It would be so much easier for me if my children would just let my conscience be their guide.

What if the Purpose of Marriage is Holiness, Not Just Happiness?

December 14, 2006

"Angelina Speaks" might have been the title of *Vogue* magazine's Angelina Jolie interview, which will hit newsstands with a splash Friday. I previewed a copy of the January piece, "The Bold and the Beautiful," by Jonathan Van Meter, photos by Annie Leibovitz.

For the first time Jolie spoke openly about her relationship with Brad Pitt, whom she met in 2004 on the set of *Mr. and Mrs. Smith*, while he was still married to Jennifer Aniston. Jolie tells *Vogue* of their growing friendship and the "joy" they found in working together and that, by the end of the movie shoot, "we just became kind of a pair. And it took until, really, the end of the shoot for us, I think, to realize that it might mean something more than we'd earlier allowed ourselves to believe."

We know the rest of the story, or a lot of it anyway. By January of 2005, Pitt and Aniston were separated, in April Pitt and Jolie were an item enjoying the sands of Africa together. Late that year Pitt and Aniston were officially divorced, and Jolie was pregnant with Pitt's child.

Cut! Let's review. This is not about Jolie and Pitt and whether or not they considered how they were impacting others. But how we have responded to them may be a Rorschach test for how we as a culture have come to value or devalue marriage.

There have been two main responses:

a) Fawning over the notion that Brad and Angelina are in love, so all is well and everybody ended up in the right place or;

b) The lesser-heard view, that Jennifer Anniston was really better for Pitt and too bad Brad can't see that.

What I have yet to hear is:

c) Pitt was married to Aniston, so "a" and "b" aren't relevant.

What a concept.

Now forget these Hollywood players altogether. Just consider what the players have revealed about our culture's view of marriage: Marriage has largely become an "as long as I'm happy in the moment" idea. One wonders then, what's the point of making the promise "to love and to cherish as long as we both shall live?" One can't promise how one will feel. One can only promise what one will do.

If keeping our spouse relies on his or her always wanting us, that's pretty unnerving! Let's face it, there are times in all of our lives when we're not exactly wantable. Being free to be ourselves, which means even being free to fail, and knowing that our spouse is committed to us anyway, is the glory of a faithful marriage. But when that faithfulness to the marriage itself is lost, everything and anything becomes an excuse to leave.

What a tragedy.

Contrary to what our culture has come to believe, a marriage is, thankfully, about something much bigger than just the two people involved. And a right view of marriage allows us to grow in character and wholeness and humanity as we learn that in marriage we are all given imperfect people to love and care for. The promises we make in marriage vows are especially for the times when we are not happy in the moment.

I don't really know anything about Brad Pitt or Angelina Jolie or Jennifer Aniston. I don't much want to. But I do know there has been a general and overwhelming response to the unfolding of events involving these movie stars that speaks to the way in which our culture both misunderstands and devalues marriage.

And in that, we are all settling for too little.

CHAPTER FIVE

Why Divorce Matters

So they are no longer two, but one flesh. Therefore,
what God has joined together, man must never separate.

Mark 10:8-9

This may be the most personal of all the chapters in this volume. Well, at least it's probably the one that hits closest to home for me.

It's simply the case that divorce matters for all the reasons that marriage does.

In the columns that follow I look at how The Church has too often in effect abandoned marriage by turning a blind eye to the divorces in its own midst. (Though that certainly was not my own experience, I'm grateful to say, and I think that made my recovery so much faster.) And the popular notion that one can leave a spouse but not a family? Well, that's just nonsense as I hope I show.

I think what will always amaze me most about divorce, though, is how many lives one divorce touches and hurts. It's never just the spouses involved. Or even the children. It's friends, children's friends, neighborhoods, grandchildren, future spouses, subsequent generations. People we don't even know. Sometimes the effects, I think particularly for children, will last a lifetime. I wish so much those pursuing divorce would pause, just for a moment, to see the pebble they are throwing into a pond and consider the ripples it might cause.

I won't even go into all the scary statistics about divorce. I will say that divorce hurts more than one imagines. And in a way, that makes sense. A married couple is literally joined together. They are one flesh. Breaking up a marriage is tearing apart that flesh. It's as simple, and as complicated, as that.

But it's also true that we often see God most at work where we are most hurt. What a gift that is. This means that even when we feel the effects of divorce, divorce doesn't have to define us. God is so gracious and redemptive. And He often chooses to make something very new, and very different, and even very wonderful of our lives when we least expect it.

When the Church Abandons the Marriages in its Midst

April 14, 2011

Once again this week, in a discussion with a friend, I found that a church had not defended marriage. How? By not defending a marriage.

The typical scenario I've seen more times than I can count goes like this: A couple are very much involved in the church, often official members. There's abandonment or adultery, and I mean openly acknowledged walking out the door for good against the other's wishes and/or a publicly displayed affair. And church leadership does essentially nothing.

I'm focused on Protestant and evangelical churches here since that's what I'm most familiar with, but I've seen it in Roman Catholic churches, too.

People in The Church divorce at the same rates as those outside of it. Enough already. The Church needs to start defending marriage. It must say: "If you join our church, we will defend your marriage." If it won't, how dare it speak to the breakdown of the family, the increased sexualization of the culture, the rise of homosexual marriage or a host of other issues it seeks to address?

There is a biblical model for church discipline and the specifics in a secular column are less important than understanding the purpose, to win back the straying party - which in a divorce may include both partners - and to stand for truth whatever happens.

Of course, when it comes to marital breakup, perhaps the one saying "enough" had good reason, say, ongoing adultery by the other. That's what church leaders are called to find out when at all possible. Once that's determined, discipline includes private attempts to reach out to the offending party or parties, and then and only if that's unsuccessful, public admonishment to the congregation. If the sin continues, the offender (s) is to be put out of the church. (Matthew 18.)

The hope is always that he or she will return, and that such discipline now will save him or her from much worse, spiritually speaking, later.

Extreme? I don't think so. Churches are voluntary organizations, and they ought to stand for something far different from the current trends of popular culture. When a church refuses to deal biblically with a divorcing couple who are members of its body, it's telling every other couple in that church that "we won't defend your family, either."

Yet I know of only a handful of divorces, including my own, where church leadership stepped in and took such biblical action to defend marriage. I do know that in these particular church bodies, divorce rates are typically much lower than in the surrounding communities or other churches.

Hopefully, in many churches, action is being quietly and successfully taken before a marriage is irretrievably broken.

In fact, true church discipline should start long before it gets to even that stage. We ought to be in churches where we are so connected, so regularly in each other's homes, enough a part of each other's lives, that we are building each other up in our relationships on a regular basis. We need to be training, teaching and encouraging in our churches. There needs to be a comfort level in approaching each other long before sin becomes flagrant. Just flitting in and out of a church on Sunday morning or Saturday night without any accountability is no way to live a biblical Christian life.

Churches should be nurturing this kind of community. And when it must follow the biblical guidelines to bring systematic discipline, church leadership must not pull back, but instead pursue the straying sheep with firm and gracious love. This is the biblical mandate given to The Church.

Look, idolizing marriage is not the goal here. Repentance and forgiveness may happen even in those instances where restoration of the marriage itself is not possible.

But in any event, defending marriage needs to start at home. So I suggest that every time we hear a pastor speak about the calamity of broken families in the culture, we should first ask:

"And just what are you doing to defend marriage in your own church body?"

From a Single Mom - It's Supposed to Take a Family to Raise a Child

April 18, 2005

After unexpectedly becoming a single mom, I had to face reality and choose a new neighborhood for my four young kids and me. It turns out I ended up in a little community with one of the highest rates of married households in the country.

And I think that's great, because I want my kids to grow up seeing what is best and good.

I thought of my situation as I read Senator Rick Santorum's best selling new book, *It Takes a Family: Conservatism and the Common Good*, in which, among other things, the distinguished gentleman from Pennsylvania makes the case for the importance of the traditional family for raising children.

Santorum lays out the statistics for what surely we already know in our hearts: The best place for a child to grow up is in a home with his married biological or adoptive mom and dad. Just because that doesn't always happen doesn't make it any less true. I think we single parents give a gift to our kids when we acknowledge that truth. We certainly don't need to run from it just because it no longer applies to our own lives. And yet I hear many divorced parents who, I think sadly, seem to feel they have to do just that.

Peggy Drexler in her new book, *Raising Boys Without Men: How Maverick Moms are Creating the Next Generation*, echoes today's cultural message when she says it literally does not matter over the long term whether or not a boy grows up with his dad living in his home. She says they will naturally find male role models elsewhere. Well, it may not matter to her, but it's a sure bet it matters in the here and now and future to the millions of boys in that situation, including mine.

Yes, some single-parent families may be healthier than some married ones, but there's a basic design for families that works best, and that's a married mom and dad under one roof. Is this really controversial?

I mean who among us, even the single parents, even Peggy Drexler, really don't care whether or not our own children grow up and get divorced?

I think of people who have told me of their experiences in having cancer. (My mom died of cancer 10 years ago and here I'm drawing on the experiences of her and her friends with cancer.) I never met anyone who said, "Having cancer is as good as being healthy." These cancer victims naturally viewed health as the ideal, whether or not they could or would fully achieve it again themselves.

But that doesn't mean these folks didn't deal positively with the condition they'd been given. In fact, some of the most amazing people I met during that time and since, those who coped best with their cancer, saw it as destructive and unnatural, *and* yet believed that somehow it was God's (difficult) plan for them at the moment. Not one of them would have chosen their cancer. But they often spoke of learning through the suffering, of coming to savor life, and every day and every blessing and every joy more fully than ever before, *because* of the adversity of the cancer.

We single parents can't give our children the gift of helping them to interpret and even grow from the adversity of divorce if we don't face it for what it is in their lives. I see so many divorced parents who seem defensive about the difficulties facing their kids, even amongst the millions who, like me, found their marriages ended against their will. Perhaps they feel they can't stand up for marriage when their own has fallen. I don't think that's true at all.

I think we single parents honor our children and we honor marriage, including the memory of our own marriage, when we admit it's the ideal and what we wanted for our own family and what we want for our kids someday. Only then can we apply wisdom and truth to our own particular situation, and encourage our kids to face and find fullness and even new sources of strength and enjoyment in the midst of the adversity they've been given.

Why Choosing to Leave a Spouse Means Choosing to Leave a Family, Too

March 8, 2012

If a wife and mother dies, would anyone suggest that she had left her husband, but not her children? Of course not.

And yet, when a spouse chooses to leave a marriage the conventional wisdom we hear all the time is that he "left his marriage but not his kids." And so for instance in the best selling book, *Helping Your Kids Cope With Divorce: The Sandcastles Way*, author Gary Newman writes, "Divorce is between parents, not parents and their children."

I doubt that many children buy that nonsense. Not least of all since divorce is typically much like a death, and of course for the children too. Even most divorce "experts" agree on that much. There's a reason it is. The way the Bible describes marriage, a divorce is very much like the ripping away of flesh itself.

Divorce naturally hurts because the marriage it involves is meant to be so foundationally important to all of the lives it encompasses.

That's also why historically there was an understanding that marriage was not just about the happiness of the two people involved. And so German theologian Dietrich Bonhoeffer, from his prison cell in Nazi Germany, famously wrote to a young bride and groom:

"Marriage is more than your love for each other. . . In your love you see only your two selves in the world, but in marriage you are a link in the chain of the generations. . . "

Even outside of a religious context marriage was intimately tied to a community and extended family, and particularly the children the marriage produced.

In recent years of course we've selfishly romanticized marriage to be about just the moment-by-moment pleasure of the two parties engaging in it. So now, people routinely have the idea that they are splitting from their spouse but not their children.

Even practically speaking this makes no sense. When a spouse leaves, he is choosing not to live with his children day by day. Or she is creating a situation where the other parent can not do so. Or, they've both decided one of them won't. In the case of adult children, the departing parent or parents are fundamentally changing how that family will interact with each other, and even its future members, for good.

Yes, when a mom leaves a husband she is no longer legally a wife, but she is (barring some unusual case) legally a mother. She no longer considers her ex as her husband, but she still sees her children as her children. Understood.

But it's no accident that synonyms of divorce are "divide," "disconnect," "split." Yep. And in divorce, that's exactly what happens to the whole family whatever the legal relationship of its members.

Interestingly, research shows that children who experience the death of a parent typically are not at risk for the poor life outcomes that children of divorce are. Yet in the case of death a parent is gone forever, and that's not usually true of divorce. The variable is not the presence or absence of a parent per se then, but how it happened. In one case there's a terrible loss. In the other, there's a loss - and a choice to split from - the whole family. And it's the latter that is typically most devastating to all the members of the family.

I'm not suggesting these things should be overtly communicated to children, as in "I'm splitting from you too. . . " I am suggesting that it's so obviously the case, we should simply recognize what so many children of divorce, of all ages, experience in real life. Kids are smart. They get it. Even those of us who unwillingly have divorce thrust upon us do our children a favor when we "get" it too.

Ahh, but where we might do things differently is in dealing with adults we love who are contemplating divorce. Every time we hear someone say, "I'm leaving my spouse - not my children," or "we are divorcing each other, not our kids" we might say something like Bonhoeffer did to that young couple: ". . .In your love you see only the heaven of your own happiness, but in marriage you are placed at a post of responsibility towards the world and all mankind."

Telling the Truth to Kids About Divorce? It's Not That Complicated!

January 21, 2010

In the hilarious romantic comedy *It's Complicated*, there's a scene in which grown children make it clear they are not happy at the prospect of their parents getting back together 10 years after their breakup. Why? "We're still getting over the divorce," one explains.

Of course they are. In fact, I'm convinced that our culture and its effort to normalize divorce make it harder for kids to heal from it.

I was reminded of this recently when talking to a dear friend whose husband also left their family years ago. We compared notes about how we've been adamantly told by the culture - from books to schools to certain counselors - to maintain to our kids that "the divorce is sad, but no one is at fault."

I've known many people over the years blindsided by a spouse choosing to leave who themselves insist on buying into this thinking. Talk about drinking the Kool-Aid. To say both parents decided to end the marriage when that's a lie is degrading to the faithful spouse. But the cover-up is supposed to help the kids - how, exactly?

In contrast, I had people in my life who encouraged me to follow a different and more honest path when my marriage ended.

Many times I've shared with friends and readers facing similar circumstances the things I've learned, observations they tell me have been helpful. Well, for those who might find it so, here are some highlights. Just beware of "cultural incorrectness":

The big picture is that it doesn't necessarily take two people to end a marriage. It can take just one who decides to break a promise and walk away from the marriage when the other spouse has remained, and desires to remain, committed to it.

Now let's get personal:

1. You weren't a perfect wife or husband by a long stretch. Ditto your spouse. It was still his or her calling to remain faithful to your marriage. That's why it's "marriage," not "dating."

2. If you tell your children that you are complicit in ending the marriage when you are not, your children will know you are lying. Then whom will they trust? What will they think of your own values and commitment? What will they think of marriage itself someday?

3. To the extent you make compassionately clear that the problem lies in the heart of the one who chose to break a promise that was to last a lifetime, the less likely your children are to blame themselves for the divorce. Almost certainly, the more likely they are to have healthy relationships later.

4. Compassion is key. We are all sinners, capable of far worse than we probably imagine. Sin can be so blinding! And so without sharing details I didn't need to, I

told my kids years ago: "Your dad didn't leave because he could see clearly, but precisely because he couldn't."

There's more, but you get the idea.

In *Complicated*, there's a poignant moment in which Dad (Alec Baldwin) is standing in a doorway and looking in on the family he left. The children, like my kids, have a relationship with their father. Still, as they sit down to dinner with their mom (Meryl Streep) and he goes home to the woman he left them for, he looks longingly and sadly at a family scene that can never truly be his again.

The whole movie hit close to home for me. But that moment made me sad for my ex's loss most of all. I think being honest with myself and with my children over the years has brought me to that redemptive place. And so I'm grateful, especially for my children's well being, that with the help of wise friends I was able to see that truth can be hard, and freeing, at the same time.

Divorce - Five Years Later, and Learning a Little Resiliency Goes a Long Way

June 18, 2009

In a few days, I'll mark the fifth anniversary of the afternoon I watched my husband finally walk out of our family life after 17 years of marriage. This time, he wouldn't return to it. The kids were 10, 8, 5 and 3.

So many folks over the years, both men and women, have shared their own similar stories of heartbreak with me. I suppose I could fill a book on the things I've learned from all this about life and people and being single with four kids.

Most importantly, from my point of view, is how my children have done with it all. I can't write their story yet. But I can tell a little piece of my own, in case it's helpful to anyone else.

Five years later, I have discovered that life goes on in incredibly wonderful if totally unexpected ways. I have found a new richness and texture and happiness in life, even amid the adversity in its many forms, as well as the joy in its many forms. When I was married and my children ran through our house chasing each other and laughing, it was music to my ears. But considering their story, when they do it now I hear new music. It's the New York Philharmonic!

Yes, there's no doubt I'm incredibly fortunate in all this, considering my many dear friends, my work, health, family, you name it. More than anything else, my Christian faith has allowed me to see my circumstances as a calling with a purpose.

I also know now there was something built into me as a child that has been instrumental in allowing me to face this. Simply put, no one ever kept me from scraping my knee as a kid.

I was the youngest of five. I wasn't protected from disappointment. Not making the school play or being left off the list for the cool girl's party - hardly traumatic in any event - was cause for dusting myself off and going on to the next thing. Not wallowing in self pity.

And I was regularly allowed to figure out things on my own or with my friends. How fast do I want to careen my bike over that edge? (Really fast.) Will that branch 20 feet high actually hold me while I eat lunch? (Yes.) How exactly do I get off the commuter train in downtown Chicago and find my dad's office in The Loop by myself - at age 10? (Seriously.)

In the summers, I was expected to be home when the streetlights came on, and not much before. That left a lot of time for successful if sometimes "dangerous" exploration. Add three wonderful older brothers who tormented me on a fairly regular basis - which did not seem to offend my parents much - and I think one has a recipe for resiliency.

So even early on in facing my new life as a single mom, even amid the grief and the loneliness and the anger, there always seemed to be an optimistic sense of "Well, okay, of course I can figure it out. In fact, it might be a kind of unexpected adventure."

I'm not sure how I'm doing yet on giving that same sense to my kids. I do know that, as a culture, we no longer typically raise resilient children built to rise to a new challenge. Too often, overprotected kids become paralyzed in the face of adversity, disappointment or loss.

Yet ironically, if our children don't become resilient adults, we leave them vulnerable after all.

I would never wish my family's loss on anyone. But I hope so much to raise children who could face similar difficult and unexpected circumstances and worse with a sense of "well, of course I can figure it out. And naturally, I'll keep a lookout for joy in the process."

CHAPTER SIX

From The Other Woman to A Marriage Transformed

Grow old with me, the best is yet to be.

Robert Browning

Over the years, I have received notes from countless husbands and wives who have had a spouse leave them. The following columns include some very personal stories of people in the midst of affairs. One, The Other Woman herself, another an unrelated story of a woman whose marriage is surviving an affair. I've found the latter to be a beautiful story of redemption.

Meanwhile, just how should we think about a website that encourages just such illicit liaisons?

By the way, I've observed that we sometimes think a cheating girlfriend or boyfriend is more offensive than a cheating spouse. Really? You'll see what I mean if you keep reading.

A word on Casey (her real name) and "Denise" (a real person but not her real name.) I am so grateful for how they opened up to me and let me get inside of their lives. Their stories speak for themselves.

I (almost) close where my own story in these pages began. And you know what? I am grateful to God that I can honestly say of myself, as I look back over the journey of these last several years, "You've come a long way, baby!"

But I am so very grateful that even that happier ending isn't the end of my story. Instead, there's now a new beginning with a wonderful man named Tom.

I've written a lot over the years about romance, and the importance of thinking clearly and rationally about it. And even after eight years of the ups and downs of being a single parent, I stand by it all. Really. I mean I *like* to think I have a lot of the answers to things. But I admit, finding myself middle-aged with four school-aged kids and yet being so in love, well it took my breath away. It made me realize life really is full of surprises. Sometimes they are quite wonderful. And sometimes, it's quite wonderful to not have all the answers we thought we did after all.

Only After Marriage do Cheating Rules Apply

December 10, 2009

The idea of engaging in "webtribution" is a little alien to me. Apparently that's the practice of defaming a so-called enemy on the Internet.

To me it just seems so public. I mean really, aren't there more subtle ways?

So I was only passingly interested in the merits of "The Dark Side of 'Webtribution,'" a recent *Wall Street Journal* story by Elizabeth Bernstein.

Bernstein focused on adults who engage in such online revenge, and the devastating consequences for victims and perpetrators. It all would have remained a yawner for me, except for the story of one woman, Renee Holder.

A few years ago Holder discovered that "dozens of her MySpace friends had received an anonymous e-mail calling her a tramp and a home-wrecker." Because Holder was pursuing a married man? No. The allegations came from her new boyfriend's ex-girlfriend.

What?

"Family members called and questioned her (Holder's) morals. ... several friends cut her off completely," Bernstein writes. So Holder painstakingly tried to explain to all who had been contacted that her boyfriend and his former girlfriend broke up months before Holder came along.

"It took me far longer to repair the damage than it took that woman to create it," she said.

I repeat. What?

Our culture is so confused. There is, or should be, relationship status in marriage alone. Because in marriage there is a meaningful and legal commitment that deserves respect.

That's why if Holder did go after a fellow while he was in a relationship with a woman, I'd say more power to her. Actually, I'd say that in general women shouldn't pursue men, but that's a different column.

If she'd won her man, she shouldn't have felt guilty about it. For him, if he'd succumbed to her pursuit, it wouldn't have meant anything other than he chose girlfriend B over girlfriend A. He might have left girlfriend A with a broken heart, but he'd have been totally within his rights as a single man to do so.

Of course, if he (or girlfriend B) had lied or deceived or misled in the process, they'd have done something very wrong. But on the merits here "cheating" in a boyfriend/girlfriend relationship isn't possible because such a relationship has no status that deserves protection.

In other words, Renee Holder had nothing to explain to anyone.

I admit that I think it's just silly when adults note on Facebook pages that they are "in a relationship with so and so" for instance. Please. Grow up and get back to me when you are engaged or married and have something to report.

More seriously, I cringe at how destructive it is to marriage in general and women in particular when Hollywood couples like "Brangelina" suggest that we should respect their live-in honies as their spouses.

Only after a wedding do all the rules change. Or at least that's when they should change because only then is a public commitment in place that is worthy of respect.

"What God has joined together let no man put asunder." We are called to put up careful boundaries around our own marriages, and to respect and protect the marriages of others. It's true that, sadly, ironically, we often don't do so in our culture. But we are certainly not called to protect anything less than marriage. In fact, to do so trivializes marriage.

Look, I've been a wife. At the moment, I'm a girlfriend. And I'm a happy one because there's a time and a place to think through a future together. But I hope I would never, ever confuse the privileges or the responsibilities of the two positions.

Our culture would be far better off, and women and children in particular far more protected, if it didn't confuse the two either.

Life is Short, So "Have an Affair" or "Work on Your Marriage"?

November 19, 2009

"Life is Short. Have an Affair." So reads the slogan for The Ashley Madison Agency website, a business devoted to helping married men and women sexually hook up with others.

With its in-your-face billboards and provocative ads, the site has been in the news the last few years. Recently I debated the merits of the site with its CEO, Noel Biderman, on *The Laura Ingraham Show.*

Biderman, who runs the best known of many websites for philandering spouses, claims to have millions of members. Whether or not that's true, I pointedly asked him how he would feel if his own wife and the mother of his young children were to become one of them.

He admitted he would be distraught. But he was also adamant that he would have to "look in a mirror" to figure out what he had done to steer her onto the path of adultery to begin with.

Wow. There are so many things about Biderman and his business one could respond to. But that comment really got my attention. Getting on the scale each evening with my husband

and asking, "Did I do enough today to keep you faithful, did you do enough for me, or not?"

No, thanks. That would be more shifting sand than I would want to live with. And what would be the point then of ever getting married in the first place?

But I don't have a spouse. I've written about this all before. Time has passed, and the healing has been wonderful. Still, when I look back on it, one thing I have not done is to "look in a mirror" and blame myself.

And not because I was a perfect spouse. But precisely because I wasn't.

Sure, I could list my shortcomings in that category. Biderman, or his wife, could certainly make a list of his faults. Should that win her a free membership on his web site?

Marriage can be so wonderful. But we are supposed to love and be faithful to our mates even when their flaws are most obvious. That's the covenant. And loving and being loved that way in return can be the wonderful instrument that God uses to shape and build our own characters.

Yes, while I believed my husband and I were building, and then at the end rebuilding our marriage, I was happy to look in a mirror and consider how to be a better wife. Naturally, if I get married again I'll look hard into that reflection and consider the same.

It just seems to me it's only when the protective bonds of the covenant are there that a spouse has the freedom to be most exposed, faults and all. And naturally that's when we have the greatest desire and ability to change and please.

But when a married person chooses unilaterally to break a covenant, no looking in the mirror by the other spouse can fix that. Because such a look can't shed light on what's broken.

There are many people who blame their spouse's (sometimes) very real faults for their own infidelity. I guess it's easier that way than looking in the mirror themselves. And with today's shallow "all about me" view of marriage, it's exactly what the culture encourages.

But say what he will, if Biderman's wife chose to use the Ashley Madison site to have an affair, I think he would have a lot of other action items on his list ahead of looking in a mirror.

Of course, neither he nor the site - nor even the other fellow - would have caused his wife's infidelity. That would have been her choice.

So I wonder if then Biderman might rethink his slogan. Maybe he would consider something like, "Life is Short. Work on Your Marriage."

Meeting The Other Woman

February 25, 2010

It's not every day you have a talk with The Other Woman. No, not my The Other Woman. Somebody else's.

It all started when I was recently driving late one night. Poking around the radio, I landed on a show about love and relationships. And there was Casey, the show's producer, giving advice to a caller. In the process, Casey talked openly about her own ongoing relationship with a married man stressing that she expects the fellow to leave his wife for her, Casey, in the months ahead. The man's wife does not know her husband is being unfaithful.

Boy, did I tune in.

I decided to do more. I called Casey a few days later. She agreed to talk with me in depth about the relationship if I didn't use her last name. She wants to protect him. I wanted to understand why she is public about her side of the affair.

I made the deal. But I quickly grew more interested in her story than in her openness.

Not because this narrative is unique - in fact, it's all too familiar. But because the bravado I heard on the radio completely disappeared when I later spoke to her at length over the phone. Casey just sounded, well, scared. And lost.

Casey, who is in her late 20s and has never been wed, has been seeing her married boyfriend for a year and a half.

Surprisingly to me, she admitted that she viewed his wife as the victim. And herself, a good person definitely making a bad choice. She told me she felt guilty about it, and at one point even made a reference to moral "blood on my hands."

But - and you knew this was coming - Casey believes that her lover and his wife both stopped putting effort into the marriage. In contrast, Casey told me that if he leaves his wife for her that she, Casey, won't ever stop trying. And so he won't cheat on her. She just knows.

But, she said, he has to make his choice because she can't live like this forever, as it's already hurting her self-esteem.

She has to keep this part of her life hidden from her parents, as she doesn't want to hurt them. While many of her friends have been supportive, some have ended their friendships with Casey over the affair.

Look, I thought I would be angry with Casey, but I found that, more than anything, I was sorry for her. This is a young, professional, intelligent woman. She would have so much to offer a great guy. Why would she settle for an inherently dishonest one? Even if she beats the long odds, and he does leave his wife and marry her, she will be looking over her shoulder the rest of her life. There are issues in every marriage. If Casey and her boyfriend end up together, theirs would just be different ones. Right now it's illicit - and exciting. But what about when it's not?

By the way, her boyfriend and his wife do not have children. If he really wanted out of the marriage, he'd be out of the marriage.

What Casey is doing is so very wrong, and at some level she knows it. But I'm not sure she knows that she's being naive, and utterly degraded. And her lover and his role in all this? That's a different column.

I didn't tell Casey my own story, or the particular heart-break of a broken marriage when infidelity is a part of it. That's not relevant here. I don't even condemn her, in the sense that I believe anyone and everyone is at least capable of being blinded by gross sin.

What I'm focusing on here is Casey the woman. That she's not just taking too much of the wrong thing, she is settling for way too little of the right thing. I still don't know why she's being open about the life she is living. I do know that, for Casey's sake, and her lover's and his wife's, I hope her dreams here don't come true.

An Affair to Forget

March 17, 2011

My friend "Denise" - not her real name - came to me in despair a few months ago. Married for more than 20 years and with children still at home, she found out her husband had been having an affair for some time.

Denise didn't listen to close family members who basically told her to kick him to the curb and start a new life on her own. That seems to be our culture's prevailing attitude as well. Instead, she is choosing to fight for her marriage because there is so much at stake.

Denise has asked me to walk with her in this, I suppose because she knows how strongly I believe she is doing the right thing. Of course, she's not doing it by herself. Her husband agreed to end the affair, and to work with her to save the marriage. That's not easy. Pulled out of a "double life" because of discovery, but not regret, suddenly being faithful again is new to him. I give him great credit for trying, instead of just walking.

Still, emotional explosions have not been uncommon between them. Of course, it's a roller coaster.

This is her story. Actually, I guess it's their story. Denise has wisely worked to limit those she's personally told. However, she agreed to let me share their struggles here - while protecting their anonymity - in the hopes this might help someone else.

Denise recently sent me a bit of her journal. She wrote that "several months in (after the discovery) and I am still here. I am still alive and I am still in my marriage trying to make it work. ... I have never been so tested in my life. I just keep trying to stay focused on how I want this sad story to have a happy ending, especially for my children."

What Denise hopes for, she told me, is real repentance over time from her husband. And it does take time for someone pulled out of serious sin to come to repentance. She eventually hopes for a new marriage with the same man.

Denise needs her husband to take ownership of what he did. In turn, he needs her to acknowledge that he's really trying to change. They found a counselor they trust. While they are digging deep at the moment, she's held out to him that she wants there to come a day, and soon, when this is put behind them for good and she does not have the right to bring it up again. Ever. That, in turn, gives him hope that he can have his family back without this hanging over him forever.

Also from her journal: "We have had some wonderful moments of intimacy that reacquaint us with the connection and love that brought us together decades ago. We have also had some wretched and painful evenings where the pain and guilt swallow us both whole."

No kidding. It's a tough road. But right now she's optimistic, and I think she has reason to be. It takes real strength, in the form of God's grace, to do what they are doing.

And this isn't over yet. Denise knows someone caught up in that life has a real chance of going back to it. "For better and for worse" they said in their wedding vows. Will her husband choose to walk that path now? Time will tell.

She'll be OK if he doesn't. They and their children will all be so much better off if he does. I have real optimism that they can repair and rebuild. But if they do, it will only be because, for starters, both of them will have turned their backs on the "it's all about me" culture.

I plan on writing more about their story. I hope, and believe it's very possible, that the next installment will be a happy, well, new beginning.

An Update on Casey: Her Married Boyfriend Divorces

September 2, 2010

When I last left off with Casey, she was in the midst of an affair with a married man. She's in her late 20s and never married, he's a few years older. They lived in different cities. Casey was growing increasingly frustrated that her boyfriend wasn't making a decision about whether to be with her or his wife.

Casey seemed scared when I first spoke with her, different from the oh-so-sure-of-herself person I'd heard discussing her affair on the radio, which is how I "met" Casey. Anyway, I wrote that her dreams of a future with her married boyfriend were unlikely to come true. And if they did, she'd be looking over her shoulder the rest of her life.

Flash forward six months, and once again Casey was willing to open up to me. A lot has changed. She'll soon have a new job and she'll be living in the same city as her boyfriend, whom, she told me, is now divorced.

I admit it: I was gobsmacked at that news. (His ex, she said, still knows nothing of Casey. There are no children involved.)

When I talked to her several months ago, Casey quietly referred to having "moral blood" on her hands. This time, needless to say, she sounded a lot happier. Casey assured me that she was not the reason for the divorce. And, in one sense, she's right. Ultimately, he was the one willing to break the promise. She was a means to his end.

But that doesn't excuse Casey in my book. Why? Because it takes a village to defend a marriage. It's a public institution we are called to protect from within and without. In something of the same way, I was better off as a kid than most are today because I knew if Mrs. Cooper or Mrs. Clancy found me up to something, they'd call my mom in a heartbeat and I'd be in big trouble.

Let's just say that offered me moral protection in weaker moments.

But marriage, tragically, has become privatized. We're redefining it to be whatever we want it to be according to our own personal happiness right now. So then, naturally, we no longer feel a responsibility to shore up, to outright protect, each other's marriages. And that leaves them more prone to falling apart in their inevitable moments of weakness.

Casey is reflecting the cultural ambivalence we have today toward marriage in general.

Still, I can tell Casey is struggling with all this. That she was raised to know better, as she told me when we first talked. Maybe that's why I admit I like her and have compassion for her. It's like she's wishing that it had all started out very differently. I don't suggest for a minute that she's not morally responsible for her choices. Only that I'm well aware that for any of us, sin of any stripe can quickly become powerful and blinding.

Anyway, what now? Well, Casey says that she and her boyfriend will date for a while in a "normal" environment where everything is out in the open. She suspects that they will eventually move in together, and after that get married.

I'm guessing her boyfriend will want to date other women now that he's single. But I was totally wrong about his divorce, so who knows? Casey says she wouldn't stand for that - if he doesn't know she's "the one," she'll walk away. She realizes her heart could still be broken. There's a long road ahead.

I'm left wondering if their life from here on out could ever be normal given how it began.

For my part, I would love to call Casey in six months and find that she's met a great guy and sees this affair, and her current boyfriend, in a very different light than she does today.

Stay tuned.

The Story of a Marriage Redeemed?

August 25, 2011

This past March, I shared with permission my friend "Denise's" story of discovering her husband's long-term infidelity. She sent me excerpts from her journal at the time, including this one: "I have never been so tested in my life. I just keep trying to stay focused on how I want this sad story to have a happy ending, especially for my children."

Denise told me she continues to feel tired and stressed, but is increasingly confident that her marriage can be made whole again. It will be a different kind of wholeness, surely, but this is where they are now: Denise's husband convinced her early on that it was his intention, at least, not to return to his affair. But there was a lot of anger on his part at first. He felt a little trapped. Still, Denise was hopeful that she would see real repentance over time.

Since then she believes that, by God's grace, she has. That he is taking real ownership of his sin, which in turn is allowing her more and more to get to the place she longs and needs to be: Where she can put the affair behind them both, and never bring it up again.

She told me that she feels a key to the ongoing healing is a structure for accountability for both of them. Meaning, for starters, seeing a counselor they both trust on a weekly basis, and attending church together every Sunday. Her husband's desire to meaningfully engage with her on several levels has, she thinks, been a basis for repair. No doubt it was and is a bellwether of his commitment to his family.

Eventually they will get to the dynamics of the marriage itself and how to make those more satisfying.

Denise told me that they have grown closer, for now, as a result of walking together through the mire. One thing that struck her? "I now have a better sense of the sin people are capable of." She's including herself there, too.

They are not "back" yet. There is still anger and frustration on both sides, and the emotions sometimes come when they least expect it. She is still scared. She knows of similar stories where things seemed promising, but then further infidelity cratered the marriage.

I like the song "Slow Fade" by the group Casting Crowns. It speaks of sin, especially infidelity, as being a process: "People never crumble in a day/it's a slow fade, it's a slow fade. . ." the lyrics go in part. I think that's true. Recovering from sin can be a process, too.

Right now, Denise is determined to do everything she can to succeed and to help her husband. He seems to desire in turn to help her. They both know they need God's grace in this.

Sure, there will be rough patches, but the couple seem to have the big picture right. That's why, unlike Casey's narrative, I believe that Denise and her husband's might become a genuine redemption story.

A Conclusion, But No Clarity, in Casey's Affair

August 4, 2011

It's long been time to touch base again with Casey.

When I first wrote about her in February 2010, the young woman was in the throes of an affair with a married man in a different city. She had been openly talking about it on the air as a radio personality. When I interviewed her privately, she was transparent with me and her brave front disappeared. She was simply scared of losing him.

Late last summer, we talked again. Much to my surprise - I wrote at the time I was "gobsmacked" - he had indeed left his wife, whom Casey believes had no knowledge of the affair. A more confident Casey was moving to his city to be with him. She told me she expected they would date for a while in the open and then get married.

All along, her vulnerability has allowed me to feel compassion for Casey the person, not just legitimate anger at her and her once-married paramour.

So it was again this time. When she agreed to speak with me recently, I assumed it was because she and the now-single boyfriend were on a smooth path. I couldn't imagine otherwise, because who wants to give anyone the opportunity to say or even think, "I told you so"?

I was surprised again. Her first words to me: "Well, he cheated on me." She said things had been lovely on the road trip together back to his city. Then there was more distance, they grew further apart and, finally, she heard from a mutual acquaintance, who did not know that he and Casey were involved, that he had a new girlfriend. And it sure wasn't Casey. She confronted him, he denied it, she figured out it was true, and she ended her relationship with him.

Casey was devastated.

What a roller coaster. I admit for purely personal reasons that I wasn't really looking forward to speaking with Casey again. I didn't want to listen to how it had somehow all "worked out."

Well, I didn't have to. And yet I find myself liking Casey. So without in any way minimizing her complicity in the affair, I can certainly be glad for her sake that she is rid of the guy at last. None of this means I'm suspending all (appropriate) judgment, by the way. It's just that one can be truly sorry that another is caught up in sin, you know.

Casey told me, "I know this is hypocritical to say, but he violated my trust." Yet, "of course he did" is not how Casey sees it. She claims that he wasn't destined to cheat just because of how their affair started. But he did, and she even told me she is resolved never to get involved with a married man again.

Still, this story doesn't have a neat little bow on top of it, either. I wanted to hear, "I so regret it all/what was I thinking/ I'm repentant." In our first conversation, Casey referred to having moral blood on her hands as a result of the affair. But she almost seemed further from that sensibility now. She told me she is not proud of her actions, but ultimately she does not regret the relationship.

Like I said, no tidy bow here. At least, not yet. Life is like that sometimes.

Meanwhile, Casey is involved with a new man, who is single. They are moving in together in a few weeks. She's told him about her affair. He is not happy about it, but believes she won't do it again. She thinks they will get married. I think in many ways Casey is still on a roller coaster, just a different one.

I will continue sharing Casey's story as long as she continues sharing it with me. And, I admit, I'll keep hoping for that tidy bow for her sake.

"Denise" and Marriage: A Story of Grace

February 2, 2012

It's been a little over a year now since my friend "Denise" (not her real name) discovered her husband's long-standing infidelity. Married over twenty years with children still at home, she experienced the betrayal like one might a hurricane.

But more than a year later, she and her husband are still standing. And they are doing it together.

Early on, Denise asked me to walk with her in this trial, and also gave me permission to anonymously share her story hoping it might help others. I first wrote about her and her husband last March when it was all as raw as fresh meat. She told me then about the anger and emotion she was experiencing. She shared with me something she had written in her journal: "... I have never been so tested in my life. I just keep trying to stay focused on how I want this sad story to have a happy ending, especially for my children."

She did stay focused, and fought for her marriage. Thankfully, her husband decided to do the same. By August, when I wrote about Denise again, things had really turned a corner. Her husband, who had taken steps to end the affair and prove to her it was over and that he had changed, had been (and still is) consistent about counseling for himself and them.

So where are they now?

Wisely, and in contrast to what the popular culture often preaches, they both believe that she does not bear any responsibility for the affair. (After all, every married person has a flawed spouse who does not fully meet his or her needs - that's the only kind of spouse there is!) But now as she sees him committed to the marriage, she's freer to enjoy pleasing him as a wife. And working to please him more.

In turn she's asking more clearly for what she needs from him as her husband.

She said that her marriage has new rhythms. He's always enjoyed the outdoors and now she is joining him in many of those pursuits, like hiking and biking. She's letting him know, much more vocally and consistently, that he is appreciated. He is more emotionally available to her. There is better connection.

She said, "Betsy, I was able to tell him on his way out the door the other day, 'I really am enjoying you' - and it's true!" Even the kids see a big difference in their marriage.

So, does she trust him? "Yes," she told me. But, she also knows she could be wrong. (Really, any of us could be about our spouse.) The healing continues.

A key for her has been not ruminating on the affair, or challenging him about it as she often did at the beginning. It's hard, she told me, but she's making huge progress. He sees the progress, and so believes he's headed for a fully restored marriage in which it never comes up again.

She has learned a few things. Denise told me that early on she kept asking people - "what are the odds we are going to survive this?" Well, she said, she quickly realized that she could increase her chances by how she behaved, and by confronting, instead of being ruled by, the feelings of self-pity and humiliation which would come crowding in.

No doubt, she said, her Christian life has sustained her through it all.

Denise also shared with me she is more careful now about who she invests time in. While she kept the circle of those who knew about her husband's affair small (wise girl) she saw some friends treat her marriage like something to be thrown away. So, she's more thoughtful about who she lets in to her life, meaning who she lets influence her, on a day-to-day basis.

I asked Denise if she's angry at her husband, not just about the betrayal but the time it's taken to heal from it over the last year. Knowing Denise, I wasn't surprised when she said, "no - because I've learned so much and grown so much. I'm a better mom and we have a better marriage." Is it all rosy? No. But she had another friend ask her recently, "why are you putting yourself through this for this guy?" And blessedly, she told me, she was able to honestly respond, "because it's so worth it."

Divorce – It Can't Happen To Me! Only, It Did

June 16, 2005

It's that time of year for wonderful wedding celebra-tions. In many ways I think that this June, after 17 years of marriage myself, I am more committed than ever to the sacredness and significance of marriage, something I've written about so many times. So then this June finds me living a terrible irony: I'm passionate about the importance of marriage, but my husband has, sadly, ended our marriage and I will soon be divorced.

Dear readers it's because my commitment to marriage, and to my husband and our children, was all real that I worked hard to save my family and to help my husband want to stay within its folds. For his sake as well as ours. I loved him. I believed we were close, and that I was loved and faithfully cherished in return.

But I was wrong. So, when he finally left, my shock and grief were total.

Yet, I know the children and I will be okay.

That's because I remember Joseph in the Bible, who could say to his brothers even after they sold him into captivity, "you meant evil against me, but God meant it for good." I fully believe that God is sovereign in this, and is even (somehow) using these terrible events for His own honor and the ultimate wellbeing of my children and me.

Already, I have been able to do a wholesome thing for my children, and with their dad's permission move my four little ones and me from Virginia to a suburb of Chicago, my home, where we have been surrounded and supported by many friends and my large family. We have started a new life in a little town with people with big hearts. I'm thankful that the children are doing well and that I have begun to find peace.

I didn't always think that would be possible. There were times as events unfolded, starting over a year ago now, that my shock, and pain and anger, were overwhelming to me. But through this ordeal, I've also come to see more than ever that sin is powerful and blinding. And in turn this has convinced me that my husband chose to leave his family not because he could see clearly, but precisely because he couldn't.

Such thinking is at odds with today's "divorce culture," which seems to consistently paint marriage break-ups as at some level rational, not wrenching and destructive (which is why it has to deny that there are so many innocent victims of divorce). In contrast, having the understanding that I do I can have genuine compassion for my husband. Compassion which is completely compatible with my appropriate anger over what he has done.

Surely, there are folks who will say, "Ha! There they go again, people like Mrs. Hart, thinking marriage is so important, and her marriage is great, and this was never going to happen to her ... " well, yes. Guilty as charged. I did think those things. Shouldn't I have? My enjoyment of my marriage, my commitment to it and to our children, and my love for my husband, were all real. And so I end where I started. Everything I ever said about the significance and sacredness of marriage - and yes, the tragedy of divorce - is true. Now it's just more tangible to me.

Yet I also know that my own tragedy does not have to define me, or my children. I don't know what the future holds. But I do know that God's mercies are new every morning, and so even now I can look forward to every new morning with increasing hope in the future.

Getting a Second Chance at First Love

May 31, 2012

I suspect some folks reading this might remember a piece I penned early in 2011, something about how it was time to take the online dating plunge. It was no accident that column followed one entitled, "Who Needs Marriage? I Do!"

Well that was January. By June, I was frustrated. About to leave the relationship website world for good, I realized the one I was on had "reupped" my credit card. Automatic renewal and all that. So, what the heck. I decided to add some photos from a speaking event I had recently done in Spain and give it one last shot. . .

Enter Tom. New to the site, he noticed one of the photos I had added: A picture of me at the bullfights in Madrid, with a particular hat, and what he claims is a smile that caught his attention.

He reached out to me. We started talking. We haven't stopped.

A few months ago now, Tom asked me to marry him. I said yes. Real fast. That smile he saw on me in the photo with the hat? Well, it's been a pretty permanent fixture ever since.

Actually, it was a fixture since just about the moment we started dating.

I've never met anyone like Tom. A brilliant scientist, he has a boyish, playful, funny side that I cherish. He is extraordinarily generous and kind. And to take on my large crew? Brave!

At the top of his field, attending my middle daughter's community theater play was his top priority one recent afternoon. Are you kidding me?

There are no games with Tom. He let me know from the beginning that he was "all in." That he was courting me. That's the definition of manly in my dictionary. Yes, the chemistry is amazing. So are the shared values, including the fact that he's a committed Christian.

In other words, he has just the qualities I wrote in that earlier column I was hoping for!

Of course, I'm writing all this as a middle-aged divorcee with four school-aged kids (24/7), and as someone who thinks the idea of "soul mates" is way overrated.

So naturally I keep saying, "Really, God? Really?"

It's tempting for me to want to pontificate here (yet again!) about how to intentionally date when you have a desire to marry or remarry. But who am I kidding? The reality is that I am incredibly fortunate. I didn't do everything right by any means, which is one of many reasons I know this is God's doing. For some reason I don't deserve He simply chose to work in my life at this time in this way, and I am so grateful.

It's been a long wait, with some false steps along the way, but Tom was worth waiting for. Maybe that's the lesson.

Of course we know that there are many challenges ahead. Eight children between us, for starters. Tom's youngest is the age of my oldest. No wonder Tom is wonderful with my kids.

Tom and I have started pre-marital counseling. We are well aware that second marriages are more likely to fail than first marriages. And we both realize that we bring with us a lot of well, interesting emotional histories. Tom, like me, was devastated by a spouse leaving his family. But though neither Tom nor I chose for our first marriages to end, we both desire to be better spouses in our second - and final! - union. And we will work hard to make that happen.

Crucially important? We see each other not as fantasies, but as the imperfect people that we are. We know that in marriage, we are given sinners to love because those are the only kind of people out there. And we agree with theologian Dietrich Bonhoeffer, who from his prison cell in Nazi Germany wrote to a young newlywed couple, "It is not your love that sustains the marriage, but from now on, the marriage that sustains your love."

Friends, over the nearly eight years I've spent as a single mom so many of you have let me know you've been praying for me. You've often let me share with you my stories and struggles, and sometimes small triumphs too. In turn, you have often shared with me your stories of parenting, and single parenting, and of love, and loss, and sometimes love again. I am grateful.

So here I happily share with you my good news, say thank you from the bottom of my heart for your support, and make a promise: This new journey of mine will naturally be the subject of many future columns!

Acknowledgements

Special thanks to my wonderful readers who provide me with endless encouragement, and have very often shared with me their own moving stories (and I am so sorry I can't personally answer all the e-mails I receive!); my very generous and supportive Scripps Howard News Bureau Chief Peter Copeland and editor, Bob Jones; my good friend and radio talk show host extraordinaire Teri O'Brien and her husband Ron who first encouraged me to do this project; my terrific brother Dennis (author of the wonderful Christmas Kindle story *Reverse Santa Claus*) who so encouraged the project as well; my fantastic life-long women friends who are such great sounding boards for me, especially when we talk about these things over really good glasses of red wine; my endlessly patient children, who first had to live with a mother who wrote a book on parenting and who now has written extensively on love and romance (ick!); and of course my dear fiancé Tom, certain to be the subject of many future columns - and the one I've been waiting for my whole life.

About Betsy Hart

Betsy Hart is a best selling author and a nationally syndicated columnist for the Scripps Howard News Service. Her column on culture and family issues, *From the Hart*, is distributed each week to hundreds of newspapers cross the country. It regularly appears in *The Chicago Sun-Times, The Boston Herald, The Washington Times*, and many other major papers.

Betsy's first book, *It Takes a Parent: How the Culture of Pushover Parenting is Hurting out Kids and What to do About It*, was released in September, 2005, and was a top seller for its publisher, Putnam Books.

The Kindle version of her newest book, *From the Hart: on Love, Loss, Marriage (and Other Extreme Sports)*, was a #1 Amazon Best Seller in "Divorce".

Betsy is a frequent guest on television and radio. She is featured on the daily "Family Minute" on WYLL radio in Chicago, and has often appeared on the FOX News Channel's *Hannity* show, *Fox and Friends*, and on other television and radio networks discussing news events of the day. Previously, Betsy served on the Reagan White House staff in the Office of Communications.

In an appearance on *The Oprah Winfrey Show*, Betsy was featured as one of America's top five women columnists.

Betsy is raising her four school-aged children in the suburbs of Chicago.

Contact Information

I welcome your feedback, and I love hearing your stories.
You can email me at: StraightfromtheHart@rocketmail.com
follow me on Facebook at: facebook.com/StraightFromTheHart
on Twitter at: twitter.com/#!/BetsyHartSpeaks
And visit my website at: www.betsysblog.com

Made in the USA
Lexington, KY
12 July 2012